IN TUNE

OTHER BOOKS BY GERALD N. LUND

NONFICTION

The Coming of the Lord

Divine Signatures: The Confirming Hand of the Lord

Hearing the Voice of the Lord:
Principles and Patterns of Personal Revelation

Jesus Christ: Key to the Plan of Salvation

Look Up, My Soul: The Divine Promise of Hope

Personal Revelation:
Receiving and Responding to the Voice of the Lord (talk on CD)

Selected Writings of Gerald N. Lund

FICTION

The Alliance

Fire of the Covenant

Freedom Factor

Leverage Point

One in Thine Hand

The Undaunted: The Miracle of the Hole-in-the-Rock Pioneers

SERIES

The Kingdom and the Crown

The Work and the Glory

The Guardian

IN TUNE

The Role of the Spirit in Teaching and Learning

GERALD N. LUND

DESERET
BOOK

SALT LAKE CITY, UTAH

Library of Congress Cataloging-in-Publication Data

Lund, Gerald N., author.
  In tune : the role of the Spirit in teaching and learning / Gerald N. Lund.
    pages cm
  Includes bibliographical references and index.
  ISBN 978-1-60907-858-4 (hardbound : alk. paper)
    1. The Church of Jesus Christ of Latter-day Saints—Education. 2. Gifts,
Spiritual—The Church of Jesus Christ of Latter-day Saints. 3. Christian education.
4. The Church of Jesus Christ of Latter-day Saints—Doctrines. I. Title.
  BX8610.L86 2013
  268'.89332—dc23   2013041812

Printed in the United States of America
Publishers Printing, Salt Lake City, UT

10   9   8   7   6   5   4   3   2   1

CONTENTS

—+>•<+—

PART I

TEACHING AND LEARNING BY THE SPIRIT

CHAPTER 1

"Go Ye Therefore, and Teach All Nations"

—+>•◄+—

A Teaching Church

On April 6, 1830, The Church of Jesus Christ of Latter-day Saints was formally organized in the Peter Whitmer cabin in Fayette, New York. In a revelation presented to the fledgling Church that day, the Lord sounded a theme that was to both direct and help define the Church. One section of the revelation was introduced by this sweeping introduction: *"The duty of the elders, priests, teachers, deacons, and members of the church of Christ."* Among other specific duties defined in the verses that follow, we find three key words: They are to *"teach, expound, [and] exhort"* (D&C 20:38, 42). This commandment is repeated twice more (see verses 46 and 59).

We learn from this very clear declaration that from the day of its founding, the Church of Jesus Christ was to be a *teaching church.* This was a charge that was repeated again and again, both to individuals and to the Church as a whole. For example:

- Part of Oliver Cowdery's calling was to "*teach . . . by the Comforter*" (D&C 28:1).
- Emma Smith was charged by the Lord "to expound scriptures, and to exhort the church, according as it shall be given thee by my Spirit" (D&C 25:7).
- Before the Church was even a year old, the Lord said: "I give unto you a commandment that . . . *ye shall teach them* [the scriptures] *unto all men; for they shall be taught unto all nations, kindreds, tongues and people*" (D&C 42:58).
- In a subsequent revelation the Lord told the missionaries to "*teach those revelations* which you have received and shall receive" (D&C 43:7).
- In that same revelation came this: "And now, behold, I give unto you a commandment, that when ye are assembled together *ye shall instruct and edify each other*" (D&C 43:8).
- Missionaries were taught that they were "not sent forth to be taught, but *to teach the children of men* the things which I have put into your hands by the power of my Spirit" (D&C 43:15).
- The charge to teach was not just for Church officers and missionaries. The Lord warned parents that if they failed to teach their children the key doctrines of the kingdom, "the *sin* be upon the heads of the parents" (D&C 68:25).
- That duty was not just to teach children the gospel but also to live it. Parents are to "*teach their children to pray, and to walk uprightly before the Lord*" (D&C 68:28).
- Less than a year later, missionaries were again told, "I send you out *to reprove the world* of all their unrighteous deeds, and *to teach them of a judgment which is to come*" (D&C 84:87).

- A few months after that came this sweeping commandment: "I give unto you a commandment that *you shall teach one another the doctrine of the kingdom. Teach ye diligently* and my grace shall attend you. . . . And as all have not faith, seek ye diligently and *teach one another words of wisdom*" (D&C 88:77–78, 118).
- In a revelation on priesthood, the Lord stated that one of the duties of presiding officers of priesthood quorums was to "*teach them according to the covenants*" (D&C 107:89).

A large percentage of the Book of Mormon focuses on how the leaders and parents in the Nephite church sought to teach their own people and the Lamanites. One has only to think of Lehi, Nephi, Jacob, King Benjamin, Abinadi, Alma the Elder and his son Alma, the sons of Mosiah and their fourteen-year mission to the Lamanites, Helaman, the mothers of the stripling warriors, Mormon, and Moroni. When the resurrected Christ came to America, He did two primary things: He taught and He ministered.

Alma the Younger's commitment to teaching was such that he resigned as chief judge. This was the highest civil office in the Nephite government at that time, somewhat equivalent to a president or a prime minister of a country. He did this because he understood that

> The *preaching of the word* had a great tendency to lead the people to do that which was just—yea, *it had had more powerful effect upon the minds of the people than the sword, or anything else,* which had happened unto them—therefore Alma thought it was expedient that they should *try the virtue of the word of God.* (Alma 31:5)

Can you imagine how such a "strategic approach" to social change would be received in our day? Should an Alma propose this in the halls of Congress, or a national parliament, or the General Assembly of the United Nations, those listening would assume the person was mad, totally insane.

At the very beginning of history, we learn that after being taught by an angel about Christ and His Atonement, "Adam and Eve blessed the name of God, and *they made all things known unto their sons and their daughters*" (Moses 5:12). That effort was continued by dozens of prophets and their wives, as well as faithful individuals and families, for the next four thousand years.

The New Testament dispensation was also highly focused on teaching. After His three-year ministry of teaching, the Savior's final charge to the Twelve was this:

> Go ye therefore, and *teach all nations,* baptizing them in the name of the Father, and of the Son, and of the Holy Ghost: *teaching them to observe all things whatsoever I have commanded* you. (Matthew 28:19–20; see also Mark 16:20)

Fulfilling the Charge

In the nearly two centuries since that day in April 1830, it is evident that members of the Church have labored long and diligently to fulfill their charge to teach the gospel. We see on every hand how much time and how many resources the Church commits to preaching and teaching the gospel. Consider the following:

- Every Sunday, in more than three thousand stakes and nearly thirty thousand local congregations, Latter-day Saints gather together to be instructed, exhorted, and taught.
- A major expenditure of the Church is building chapels and

meetinghouses. This is done primarily so that the Latter-day Saints have a place to gather together for worship and instruction.

- Since the beginning of the Restoration, more than a million missionaries have been sent into the world to teach and preach the gospel. Currently, there are about 80,000 full-time missionaries, organized into 405 missions, laboring in more than 150 countries across the globe.

- Before beginning their full-time service, missionaries attend one of fifteen missionary training centers around the world to be taught and trained so they can more effectively fulfill their callings. It is an enormous undertaking and quite remarkable when we consider the time, effort, and resources required to take the gospel to the world.

- And while we are talking about resources, here is another indicator of the commitment to teaching. Currently a full-time missionary from the United States is asked to pay $400 per month for his or her full-time missionary service. (Costs for missionaries from other countries and for senior missionary couples vary.) With the tens of thousands of missionaries serving each year, those personal and family costs alone run into millions of dollars every month.

- At this time, there are 141 operating temples throughout the world, with another 29 in planning or under construction. In the house of the Lord, worthy members receive sacred ordinances and are given special instruction in doctrine.

- The Church uses one of the world's most extensive nongovernmental satellite broadcasting systems to carry its message to members scattered across the globe. General conference, which is essentially ten hours of intensive instruction, teaching, and exhortation, occurs twice every year. Multistake conferences and worldwide training broadcasts are also sent out over the satellite system on a regular basis.

- The Church maintains a number of general Internet websites, including lds.org and mormon.org. Many individual congregations also maintain a presence on the web. Conferences and other events are streamed live and are made available for later use. Social media sites such as Facebook, Twitter, LinkedIn, and Pinterest are utilized to extend our outreach to members and to those not of our faith.

- In addition to regular Sunday meetings, there are stake and ward conferences, pageants, firesides, conferences, seminars, and workshops held on a regular basis.

- The Church maintains numerous historic sites that honor our heritage and provide visitors the opportunity to learn more of our history and feel "a spirit of place" where significant events occurred.

- The Church Educational System includes three major universities, a business college, and several other local Church schools. In its global system of seminary and institute programs, religious instruction is provided in weekday classes to about three-quarters of a million students. The effort and costs required to maintain these programs are enormous.

- Printed materials designed to help in the teaching and instruction process include monthly Church magazines—in English, one for adults, one for youth, one for children; and a combined international version printed in numerous languages. In addition, curriculum and training materials for all ages are prepared and distributed, many at no cost to the member.

- In addition to preparing curriculum materials for teachers and handbooks for priesthood and auxiliary leaders, the

Church prepares materials on how to be more effective in our teaching. For example, back in 1999 the First Presidency sent out a letter initiating a Churchwide effort "to revitalize and improve . . . gospel teaching in homes and in Church meetings and help nourish members with the good word of God."[1]

- That emphasis and support for improving the quality of gospel teaching in families and throughout the Church continues today. In January 2013, Aaronic Priesthood, Young Women, and youth Sunday School classes began using new curriculum materials. In the letter announcing this new curriculum to the Church, the First Presidency noted that "the focus is on strengthening and building faith, conversion, and testimony."[2]

- The Church also produces movies, videos, and other audio and visual resources for the instruction and edification of Church members and to help carry our message to the world.

- This "media outreach" includes BYUtv, which is now carried by about 600 cable TV providers in North America, making it available to about 50 million viewers. It is also available on the Internet.

There are other examples, but these suffice to show the extensive and intensive efforts of the Church to fulfill its charge to "teach all nations." These programs and materials represent quite an astonishing commitment.

Summary

In light of these things, I think we can safely conclude that:

- from the Fall of Adam to the present day;

- in every age and every dispensation;
- to every nation, kindred, tongue, and people;
- using every appropriate means and delivery system available;
- as a general Church, as quorums, as Church auxiliaries, as the Church Educational System, and as individuals and families, the call and the charge are resoundingly clear: "Teach ye diligently and my grace shall attend you, that you may be instructed more perfectly" (D&C 88:78).

The purpose of this book is to examine how we can more faithfully and effectively fulfill that charge so that someday we too may hear these stirring words from Him whom we worship:

Well done, thou good and faithful servant: thou hast been faithful over a few things, I will make thee ruler over many things: enter thou into the joy of thy lord. (Matthew 25:21)

CHAPTER 2

"If Ye Receive Not the Spirit Ye Shall Not Teach"

—▸•◂—

What to Teach and How to Teach It

A closer look at the scriptural references given in the previous chapter shows that not only has God clearly commanded us to teach, but He has also defined what we are to teach:

- Teach according to the covenants.
- Teach the peaceable things of the kingdom.
- Teach the revelations.
- Teach others how to act and direct the Church.
- Teach the things that "I have put into your hands."
- Teach children repentance, faith, baptism, and the gift of the Holy Ghost.
- Teach children to pray and to walk uprightly before the Lord.
- Teach of a judgment that is to come.
- Teach the doctrine of the kingdom.
- Teach one another words of wisdom.

A closer examination of that list also reveals the Lord's counsel on *how* we are to teach. We are to teach:

- by the Comforter.
- by the power of the Spirit.
- diligently.

The Law of the Church

There are two significant scriptural passages on teaching that were not included in the list in chapter 1. Both come from the Doctrine and Covenants. I held them back for this chapter because they are unique in that they give further clarity to our charge to teach.

Section 42 of the Doctrine and Covenants was given before the Church was yet a year old. It is referred to as "the law" of the Church (D&C 38:32; 41:3; 42:2). The revelation is filled with doctrine, principles, commandments, and counsel for the fledgling Church. In a very real sense, it served as a Church handbook of instructions in those early years. In that context, one could say that one of the "laws" given at that time could be designated as the *law of teaching* for the Church:

> And again, the elders, priests and teachers of this church shall *teach* the principles of my gospel, which are in the Bible and the Book of Mormon, in the which is the fulness of the gospel. And they shall observe the covenants and church articles to do them, and *these shall be their teachings,* as they shall be directed by the Spirit. And the Spirit shall be given unto you by the prayer of faith; *and if ye receive not the Spirit ye shall not teach.* (D&C 42:12–14)

From this single passage we learn:

- *What* we are to teach—the principles of the gospel, "the covenants and church articles."
- *What* is required of teachers as they teach—to live "the covenants and church articles."
- *How* we are to teach—by the Spirit.
- *How* to receive the Spirit—by the prayer of faith.

President Harold B. Lee specifically referred to this passage as a *law* to teachers:

> Read again what the Lord has said. I might call it the "law to the teachers." It is contained in Doctrine and Covenants 42:11–14. Here is given the four things essential to the teacher. First, he must have authority. [Second,] we are counseled as to what to teach. He said, "You shall teach the gospel as contained in the Bible and in the Book of Mormon." He does not mention the Doctrine and Covenants nor Pearl of Great Price because at that time, of course, there were no such books. Today, if the Lord were repeating it, He would undoubtedly say, "Preach my gospel as contained in the standard Church works." [Third,] He tells us how to prepare to teach. He says we shall not only teach them but we shall do them, suggesting that no teacher can teach a principle that he himself does not subscribe to and practice. And then finally, "And the Spirit shall be given unto you by the prayer of faith; and if ye receive not the Spirit ye shall not teach." That, to me, is the watchword to the teacher. That is your preparation. Authority to teach, what to teach, your own personal individual preparation to teach, and finally humbling yourself to get the Spirit of the Holy Ghost.[1]

I take this verse to mean not only that we should not teach without the Spirit, but also that we really cannot teach without it. Learning of spiritual things simply cannot take place without the instructional and confirming presence of the Spirit of the Lord.

Howard W. Hunter,
Teachings, 209

It should be noted here that "Ye *shall not teach*" can be interpreted in two ways. First, it can be read as a declarative sentence—that is, the Lord is stating that if we do not have the Spirit, we will not teach in a way that is pleasing to Him. It's like saying, "If you don't have the Spirit, you won't do any real teaching."

But it can also be read as an imperative sentence or a commandment. In other words, "If you don't have the Spirit with you, then *don't* teach." Either meaning seems to have significance for us and should give us all something to consider with great soberness.

Teach to Edify

The second significant passage of scripture that we did not include in our list in chapter 1 comes from a revelation given to the Church just a few months later. Though this was given specifically to missionaries, it is evident this counsel also has universal application for all men and women who are called to serve in the kingdom.

Wherefore, I the Lord ask you this question—unto what were ye ordained? *to preach my gospel by the Spirit,* even the Comforter which was sent forth to teach the truth. Verily I say unto you, he that is ordained of me and sent forth to preach the word of truth by the Comforter, in the Spirit of truth, doth he preach it by the Spirit of truth

14

or some other way? And *if it be by some other way it is not of God.* (D&C 50:13–14, 17–18)

There it is. In six simple words we are given our charge, our duty, our obligation as disciples: *Preach my gospel by the Spirit.* And the Lord reiterates this in another seven equally clear words: *Preach it by the Spirit of truth.* That charge is followed by these humbling and sobering words: If we try to do it in any other way, *it is not of God.* It doesn't get much clearer than that.

Following the giving of the charge, the Lord then explained *why* this manner of preaching and teaching is so important:

> Therefore, why is it that ye cannot understand and know, that he that receiveth the word by the Spirit of truth receiveth it as it is preached by the Spirit of truth? Where-fore, he that preacheth and he that receiveth, *understand one another,* and *both are edified* and rejoice together. And *that which doth not edify is not of God,* and is darkness. That which is of God is light; and he that receiveth light, and continueth in God, receiveth more light; and that light groweth brighter and brighter until the perfect day. (D&C 50:21–24)

When we preach or teach in the manner here defined, both teacher and learner understand each other, and both are edified and enlightened. They rejoice together. That is a primary goal of teaching in the Church: to edify and give light to others, to push back the darkness, to bring joy and rejoicing. To put it another way, this is *why* we stress teaching so much in the Church. This is the end result we are striving for. Only as edification happens—to us as individuals, to families, and to the Church itself—are we able to move forward. As we are edified, we gain more and more light

15

and knowledge until we reach that "perfect day" when we return to the presence of God to live with Him forever.

That is what this is all about. That is our ultimate goal, and anything less falls short of God's purposes for us.

THE HOLY GHOST AS A TEACHER

These two scriptures, which are foundational scriptures on teaching the gospel, have something in common. Both specifically and forcefully speak about the role of the Holy Ghost in teaching and preaching. In Section 42, we are told that our teachings "shall be directed by the Spirit," we are taught how to get that Spirit (by the prayer of faith), then we are specifically commanded, "If ye receive not the Spirit ye shall not teach" (D&C 42:13–14).

In D&C 50:14–23, we find reference to the Holy Ghost, the Comforter, or the Spirit of truth eight different times. And clearly it is the Spirit that edifies, which is the end goal of all teaching in the Church.

This does not surprise us, of course. We know that the third member of the Godhead does not have a body of flesh and bones like the Father and the Son. He is a "personage of spirit" so that He can dwell with us (see D&C 130:22). All three members of the Godhead act in perfect unity, but each has unique roles as well. The Father devised the plan of salvation and fathered all of us in the premortal existence. It is to Him that we pray and to Him that all honor, glory, and reverence are given.

Jesus Christ was the Creator under the direction of the Father. He was the God of the Old Testament, known as Jehovah, before He came to earth. He became mortal so that He could work the Atonement and save all mankind from death. He also taught men how to return to the Father through Him and gain eternal life.

What we know of the Holy Ghost suggests that His primary

role is to support the Father and the Son in their work and to serve as a revelator of God to man. In His calling, He fulfills many roles and functions. He testifies. He comforts. He enlightens. He reveals truth. He warns and protects from both physical and spiritual dangers. He helps sanctify and cleanse us from sin. He strengthens, fills us with hope, and confirms others' testimonies. He extends His many gifts to us, increasing our capacity as well as our knowledge and understanding. These are only a few of the things He does. As a member of the Godhead, He is infinite in His powers and endless in His functions, and the finite mind cannot possibly comprehend all that He is and does.

But one more thing is indelibly clear from what the scriptures teach us about the Holy Spirit: *He is a Teacher.* In so many ways, that is what He does. He teaches. He does this by revealing truth, testifying of truth, confirming truth, enlightening the mind. He enhances faith, pricks us with guilt and shame when we do things that displease the Father and the Son, softens the heart so we can repent, strengthens our courage as we carry out Their will, and comforts us when the burdens of life weigh in upon us. All of those work

> *[The Holy Ghost] is a reminder and will bring to our remembrance the things which we have learned and which we need in the time thereof. He is an inspirer and will put words in our mouths, enlighten our understandings and direct our thoughts. He is a testifier and will bear record to us of the divinity of the Father and the Son and of their missions and of the program which they have given us. He is a teacher and will increase our knowledge. He is a companion and will walk with us, inspiring us all along the way, guiding our footsteps, impeaching our weaknesses, strengthening our resolves, and revealing to us righteous aims and purposes.*
>
> SPENCER W. KIMBALL,
> *TEACHINGS,* 23

to teach us of the love of God and the perfect saving grace of the Godhead.

There is much to say about the Holy Ghost, but in this book, we are going to focus on this particular aspect of His nature and character. We are going to talk about the Holy Ghost as our Teacher and about what we can do to link up with Him in partnership as we seek to teach and influence others.

CHAPTER 3

TEACHING, PREACHING, AND EDIFYING

—•>•◦•<•—

SOME DEFINITIONS

Before moving further with our discussion of our desired partnership with the Holy Ghost as *the* Teacher, it would be well if we paused for a moment to define three terms we saw used in those two foundation scripture passages discussed in the last chapter. They are:

- Teach
- Preach
- Edify

TEACHING AND PREACHING

In section 42 of the Doctrine and Covenants, we are told that we must teach by the Spirit. In section 50, we are commanded to preach by the Spirit. Both of these passages remind us that the Holy Ghost is our Teacher. Do those two words, *teach* and *preach*, have different meanings, or are they synonymous and interchangeable? Although they are nearly synonymous, and often are used interchangeably, there is an important difference in the two words that we need to understand. Since both words are found in the New Testament, an examination of the Greek words that are translated as *teach* or *preach* can help us better understand that difference.

Teach

Teach comes from the Greek *didasko* (pronounced de-DAS-ko). That Greek word is almost always translated as some form of *teach*. It means "to hold discourse with others in order to instruct them; . . . to impart instruction, instill doctrine, . . . to explain or expound a thing, to teach one something."[1] Our English word *didactic*—which describes something meant to instruct—comes directly from the Greek. So when we see *teach* in the New Testament, it carries the same meaning there as it does for us today.

Preach

Unfortunately, that is not true of *preach*. *Preach* in modern English has taken on some different connotations from how it was used originally. It is most frequently associated in our minds with ministers of various Christian denominations. Often the word brings to mind the "evangelical preachers" we see on television or hear on the radio. We also use the word to describe someone who shares some supposed truth with great fervor—for example, "My doctor is always preaching to me about the importance of diet and exercise." And sometimes we use it negatively, as in "Stop preaching to me." That is unfortunate, because in the New Testament it is a very positive concept.

When we find the word *preach*, or one of its forms, in the New Testament, in the vast majority of cases it comes from one of two Greek words.

The first is *kerusso* (pronounced kay-ROOS-so). Its primary meaning is "to be a herald, to officiate as a herald; to proclaim after the manner of a herald; always with the suggestion of formality, gravity and an authority which must be listened to and obeyed." It is "used of the public proclamation of the gospel and matters pertaining to it, made by John the Baptist, by Jesus, by the apostles and other Christian teachers."[2]

Kerusso is found sixty-one times in the New Testament. While the King James translators translated it as "preach" in its various forms fifty-one of those times, in a few cases they translated it as "publish" or "proclaim."

The other Greek word that is translated as "preach" is even more instructive. It is *euaggelizo* (pronounced yoo-ang-ghel-ID-zo).[3] It is a combination of the prefix *eu* and the root *aggelos.*

Eu placed at the beginning of a word adds the meaning of "good" or "well." It is still found in such English words as the name *Eugene* (which means well born); *eulogy,* a speech praising the good qualities of another; and *euphoria,* a good feeling.

The root *aggelos* (ANG-el-os) is our word "angel." Although the primary definition of *angel* today is "a heavenly being," that is not the base meaning of the word. The primary meaning of the Greek is that of "a messenger, envoy, one who is sent."[4] It came to refer to heavenly beings because they were God's messengers.

When the prefix and root are combined into *euanggelizo,* which is a verb, we have a word that literally means "to bring good news, to

As agents of the Lord we are not called or authorized to teach the philosophies of the world or the speculative theories of our scientific age. Our mission is to preach the doctrines of salvation in plainness and simplicity as they are revealed and recorded in scripture.

JOSEPH FIELDING SMITH,
IN CONFERENCE REPORT,
OCTOBER 1970, 5

announce glad tidings." In both the Old and New Testaments, this can be used of any kind of good news, but it is particularly used of "the joyful tidings of God's kindness, in particular, of the Messianic blessings; . . . of the glad tidings of the coming kingdom of God, and of the salvation to be obtained in it through Christ."[5]

Euaggelizo is found fifty-five times in the New Testament. It is translated as "preach" twenty-three times; "preach the gospel" twenty-two times; "bring good tidings" twice; "show glad tidings" twice; "bring glad tidings" once; and "declare" or "declare glad tidings" twice. (There are three other miscellaneous uses that are not relevant here.)

"Good news," "glad tidings," and "joyful tidings" should immediately bring to mind another word: the *gospel.* We know that the word *gospel* literally means "good news" or "glad tidings." Therefore, it should not surprise us that the Greek word that is translated as "gospel" is *euaggelion,* the noun form of the verb *euaggelizo.* This word, or one of its forms, is found about two hundred times in the New Testament.

> *If there is any truth of salvation that Deity has made imperishably clear, it is that first and last, in all ages, now and forever, among the learned and the ignorant for all races and peoples, and for that matter on all the endless worlds of the great Creator, there is one formula and one formula only for conveying saving truth to men—Preach by the power of the Spirit.*
>
> BRUCE R. MCCONKIE,
> DOCTRINAL NEW TESTAMENT
> COMMENTARY, 2:318

So, although teach and preach are closely related concepts and may often be used interchangeably, there is a subtle but important difference between them:

- To *teach* carries the primary idea of *instruction and explanation.* For example, in D&C 88:77–79, early members were told to teach the doctrines of the kingdom, but they were also to teach and study such things as astronomy, geology, history, and political science.

- To *preach* is to *declare,* to *pronounce,* and to *proclaim* a specific message, namely, the glad tidings of the gospel of Jesus Christ. It is a declaration and testifying of the truth by those called to do so by God.

In His role as Teacher, the Holy Ghost both teaches and preaches, and He helps us to do the same. Throughout this book, most of what we say about the role of the Holy Ghost will refer to both preaching and teaching. Therefore, to avoid becoming tedious and saying "preaching and teaching" every time we refer to them, one word or the other will be used, even though both are often implied. Where *preaching* is used in its specific meaning, it will be noted.

EDIFYING

In section 50 of the Doctrine and Covenants, we are taught very forcefully that if what we teach and preach does not edify, it is not of God. We said that this is the "why" of our teaching and preaching. If that is so, then it is important that we also understand the richness of the word *edify*.

Most dictionaries define *edify* as meaning to strengthen or uplift someone morally and spiritually. But here again, an examination of the word's origins—in this case, its Latin roots—greatly enriches our understanding.

The verb *edify* comes from the Latin *aedificare* (pronounced ee-de-fe-CAHR-ee), which means "to build, erect, or construct." But what that definition

> *Let us therefore follow after the things which make for peace, and things wherewith one may edify another.*
>
> ROMANS 14:19

23

does not specify is that the first part of the word comes from the Latin *aedis,* which means "a temple, shrine, or tomb," that is, a sacred building.[6] Thus, directly related to the word *edify* is the word *edifice,* which is a building that is particularly impressive, splendid, or beautiful.

What a wonderful metaphor! When someone is edified, it is as if a spiritual temple, an edifice, is being constructed in the person's heart. This is why edification is the end goal of all our teaching and preaching. We teach and preach to help individuals and families and congregations and quorums and classes (and readers of the printed word) become more spiritual, more obedient, more faithful, more hopeful. This is *why* we are called to teach and preach the gospel.

The Holy Ghost Edifies and Strengthens

From section 50 we learn several important truths. First, if we wish the companionship of the Holy Ghost, *the* Teacher, as we teach or preach, we must do it by the Spirit of truth. If we do it some other way, even if what we teach is true, it will not be of God. Second, when we do preach by the Spirit, both the preacher and the listener are edified. Third, everything the Father and the Son do is for our edification—to lift and build us spiritually. Therefore anything the Spirit does in carrying out Their will brings edification. That is why the Lord so clearly states, "That which doth not edify is not of God, and is darkness" (D&C 50:23).

However, we who teach—teachers, missionaries, Church leaders, parents—often get discouraged because it seems like our efforts to edify are not bearing fruit in those we teach. Those people may seem to be ignoring or even rejecting our efforts to strengthen and uplift them. But that is why I love the metaphor of building a structure within people. In the very metaphor, we find hope and encouragement to continue on.

Nothing Is Happening

When a family contracts to have a new home built, it is an exciting time for them. They all gather to watch the tractor dig out the basement. In a matter of hours, a place is made for the new building. Then the footings go in, followed by the basement walls.

In those first weeks, almost every day, some dramatic changes take place. The flooring goes on. Walls seem to spring up, and soon the house is framed. Rafters and trusses appear overnight, and soon the house has a roof and windows.

And he gave some, apostles; and some, prophets; and some, evangelists; and some, pastors and teachers; For the perfecting of the saints, for the work of the ministry, for the edifying of the body of Christ.

Ephesians 4:11-12

But there comes the day when the outer construction is done and the house is what contractors call "dried in." Now comes the plumbing and the electrical work. This is a very different stage of construction. These are not highly visible efforts. Often what happens goes unseen by the casual observer. In this phase, it is not uncommon to hear comments such as, "Nothing is happening," or "The work has stopped." Of course, that is not true. The wires and plugs and switches and pipes are just as essential to the home as are the walls and floor, but they are small or hidden within the walls and therefore often go unnoticed.

One other aspect of the building metaphor is appropriate here. A home is built brick by brick, board by board, nail by nail, one light switch or electrical plug at a time. So it is in teaching.

Wouldn't it be wonderful if a child or a student or a Church member were to exclaim, "Wow! You totally changed my life today." We do find examples of very dramatic changes in some individuals—the Apostle Paul, Enos, Alma the Younger, King Lamoni—but those are the rare exceptions. Typically, the individuals themselves don't recognize the small, incremental building blocks being put in place as their spiritual edifice grows and expands. So it shouldn't surprise us as teachers and counselors when we think that "nothing is happening."

As Elder Neal A. Maxwell once said, "Trying to observe the slow shift from self-centeredness to empathy is like trying to watch grass grow."[7] The Lord taught the same principle in these words: "Seek the face of the Lord always, *that in patience* ye may possess your souls, and ye shall have eternal life" (D&C 101:38).

You're Not Alone

One more note about the power of this metaphor. Constructing a home or a building is a complex process involving many different aspects and a wide variety of materials. But it also is rarely done by a single individual. It requires the varied skills of architects or designers, engineers, surveyors, excavators, carpenters, masons, plumbers, electricians, roofers, landscapers, and so on. So it is with our teaching of the gospel. This too is a complex process, requiring the input of many people over an extended period of time. Even parents, who have such a major role in teaching, are not left alone. Efforts to edify come from many different sources.

Most important, we must always remember that *we* are not the primary architect, craftsman, or builder. This is the Father's work. This is why He chose His Only Begotten Son and sent Him down to earth. This is why He gives us the gift of the Holy Ghost and the power of the priesthood. This is why we have prophets, seers, and revelators; four canonized books of scripture; Relief Society,

Primary, and Young Women; seminaries and institutes of religion; weekly sacrament meetings; ward, stake, and general conferences; and so on.

All are engaged in the work of building spiritual edifices in the hearts of men, women, and children everywhere. We are not alone in this effort. The edification of the human soul is the work of God and the work of the kingdom. So let us not get discouraged and think that nothing is happening or that it is totally up to us.

That simply is not so. And the closer we draw to the Spirit, who is our Teacher and the real Teacher of those we teach, the more it simply will not be so.

I have often said that The Church of Jesus Christ of Latter-day Saints is organized love and organized concern. We need the saving ordinances administered in an authoritative way, and we need each other. One of the genius features of the gospel is that it does not permit us to escape from our brothers and sisters. We do not draw closer to our brother by pushing others away from us. We are also more effective by joining together in administering help and aid rather than being a frail force for random goodness in the world.

NEAL A. MAXWELL,
DEPOSITION OF A DISCIPLE, 60

CHAPTER 4

TEACHING BY THE SPIRIT—
A WORKING DEFINITION

—+>•<+—

MISCONCEPTIONS ABOUT TEACHING BY THE SPIRIT

As noted in chapter 1, over the last few years the Church has given renewed emphasis and attention to teaching in the Church. The movement is away from curriculum materials that are very prescriptive in saying how a lesson should be taught. Now the focus is more on principles and the individual needs of students, which are best met as the Spirit is present in the teaching setting. This is particularly evident in the new curriculum materials for youth introduced in 2013, titled "Come, Follow Me."

But there are many questions about exactly what it means to teach by the Spirit, as well as some common misunderstandings. For example, here are some statements I personally have heard people make about teaching by the Spirit:

- If a teacher is really teaching by the Spirit, even small children will sit quietly during the lesson. (Statement made by a stake Primary president in a stake auxiliary training meeting)

- We had such a great class today. We all felt the Spirit so strongly, I cried all the way through it. (Seminary student)
- I don't think it's right to use humor in our lessons because it is light-mindedness and actually offends the Spirit. (Institute teacher)
- I didn't have time to prepare a lesson; I guess I'll have to teach by the Spirit today. (Seminary teacher and many others)
- I'm not interested in all these teaching methods; I just want to teach by the Spirit. (Full-time missionary)
- I think a good test for deciding whether I'm teaching by the Spirit is if my students like me and the class. (Early-morning seminary teacher)
- I recently had a talk all prepared, but when I stood up, I felt impressed to put it aside and teach something entirely different. So now I'm wondering if I should prepare talks in advance. (Priesthood leader)
- In my religion class we don't have prepared lessons. We have an opening prayer, then the teacher has us sit quietly and wait for the Spirit to indicate what we should discuss that night. (Institute student)
- A major part of my calling is to give my girls their own spiritual experiences. (Young Women adviser)
- If I come out of my lesson feeling discouraged or downhearted, then I know that I haven't taught by the Spirit. (Seminary teacher)
- My companion and I tract "by the Spirit," meaning we walk down the street, or sometimes just stop, and wait for the Spirit to tell us where to go or what to do. (Full-time missionary)

Some of those statements, though given with good intentions, are just plain wrong for reasons we shall discuss further in the chapters to come. Some are true statements in some specific circumstances, but turning them into "general rules" becomes problematic. Our purpose here will be to try to sort out what principles we can use to guide us as we seek to learn how to more effectively teach and preach by the Spirit.

Questions about Teaching by the Spirit

Before we look at some of the common questions about teaching by the Spirit, let me pause a moment to make this clarification. When we speak of the "learner" or the "student" in this book, those terms include students in a whole host of teaching settings—formal classes, parents teaching in the home, speakers teaching in general meetings, leaders counseling members in one-on-one settings, or even two individuals conversing informally with each other.

In that same vein, when we speak of a "teacher" or an "instructor," that includes anyone trying to impart the gospel to another person or persons. With that in mind, here are some key questions we should ask ourselves about what it means to teach by the Spirit:

1. What is it that a teacher does when he or she is teaching by the Spirit? Will a teacher always know if he or she has taught by the Spirit? Will the learner?
2. What will the learner be experiencing or feeling if a teacher *is* teaching by the Spirit?
3. Is it possible that the Holy Ghost may *not* be present in a teaching setting but the teacher or learner thinks that He is?
4. Can a teacher really create a true spiritual experience for the learner?
5. For that matter, what constitutes a "true spiritual experience" for an individual?

6. Can a teacher be teaching by the Spirit and yet it has no effect, or even a negative effect, on the student?

7. Can the learner be taught by the Spirit even if the teacher doesn't have the Spirit?

8. What can a teacher do to create a climate in which the likelihood of teaching by the Spirit is increased?

These and other questions raise important issues. To answer them, we need to define clearly what we mean by teaching by the Spirit.

Teaching by the Spirit: A Definition

Many years ago, a professor in a class on logic made this observation:

> Many arguments result from the lack of clear definitions of what key terms mean. Even if two people may not agree on what is the best definition, understanding how the other person defines a word goes a long way to clarifying the discussion.

Therefore, before we can successfully attempt to answer the above questions and clear up some of those misconceptions, we need to have a clear definition of what it means to "teach by the Spirit." This is not a simple task. Teaching by the Spirit is not a tangible object that one can pick up and examine, or measure, or put on display for others. It is a process that is highly complex and has dozens of variables. In some ways, like other aspects of revelation, it is beyond the power of the tongue to adequately describe.

What follows is what I shall call a "working definition" of teaching by the Spirit. It may not adequately or ultimately define all the workings of the Spirit, but hopefully it will suffice to give us a common ground for discussing the topic. So here is my definition:

Teaching by the Spirit takes place when the Holy Ghost is fulfilling His role and His functions with either the teacher or the learner or both.

Several of the misleading statements listed above try to define teaching by the Spirit in terms of what teachers or learners are doing or feeling. But that approach suggests that somehow they are the ones who control the functioning of the Spirit. That simply is not so. The Spirit is a member of the Godhead. The Holy Ghost operates and functions under the direction of the Father and the Son. We do not *control* the Spirit in any sense of the word. We can do things that encourage the Spirit to draw closer, or to withdraw, but what He does, and how He does it, is always the Spirit's choice.

Teaching with inspiration means seeing and taking advantage of every special teaching moment that comes along or that can be purposely created.

L. TOM PERRY,
"IF YE RECEIVE NOT THE
SPIRIT YE SHALL NOT TEACH," 34

With that definition, we will turn our attention in part II of this book to a second question that naturally flows from it: *What are the roles and functions of the Holy Ghost that are directly related to teaching?*

PART II

THE FUNCTIONS OF THE HOLY GHOST

CHAPTER 5

THE HOLY GHOST EDIFIES, STRENGTHENS, AND TESTIFIES

—⊷•⊰—

THE NATURE AND ROLE OF THE HOLY GHOST

In this and following chapters, we will focus on the role and functions of the Holy Ghost as Teacher, functions that are *directly related* to the process of teaching and preaching the gospel. Here are some ideas that will be helpful as we move forward with this study.

First, there are other functions of the Holy Ghost that are not directly related to the process of a "teacher" interacting with a "learner" through teaching or preaching. Teaching may be going on between the Spirit and an individual without a third person being directly involved. For example:

- One of the major functions of the Holy Ghost is to sanctify and cleanse us from sin (see, for example, 3 Nephi 27:20; Moroni 6:4; D&C 19:31).
- The Holy Ghost warns us of spiritual or physical dangers;

this often occurs when we are alone and not in any kind of a teaching setting.

- The Spirit often gives us inspiration and enlightenment independent of any kind of formal teaching or learning setting.

- The Holy Ghost is the Comforter. While comfort can come from the influence of another person, it frequently comes directly to us from the Spirit.

These other functions obviously involve edification of the individual, but again, our purpose here is to look at interactions between teachers and learners in which the Spirit is functioning.

Second, as we look at these functions of the Holy Spirit, we shall give a few scriptural references. In almost every case, these are only a sampling of what the scriptures teach.

Third, we will examine ten functions of the Holy Ghost. This is not meant to be an exhaustive list. As a member of the Godhead, the Holy Ghost is an infinite and perfect Being, and His roles and functions are infinite as well.

Finally, I shall try to give an example or two from the scriptures, from my own experience, or from the experience of others to illustrate each specific function.

Function 1: The Holy Ghost Edifies and Strengthens

This aspect of the Holy Ghost's teaching work was discussed in some detail in chapter 3 as part of our general introduction to teaching by the Spirit. I list it again here as a reminder that it is one of the major functions of the Holy Spirit, but will not expand on it further.

FUNCTION 2: THE HOLY GHOST TESTIFIES

When we talk about what the Holy Ghost does, it is difficult to say which of all His functions is the most important. But this much we can say: His role as Testifier would certainly be one of the most important functions He has that is directly related to His role as Teacher. During the process of our teaching or preaching the gospel, the Holy Ghost consistently and constantly testifies of the truth. His is a confirming witness of the Father and the Son and of the plan of salvation and all that is included therein.

President Spencer W. Kimball said: "There are three Gods: the Eternal Father, Elohim, to whom we pray; Christ or Jehovah; and the Holy Ghost, *who testifies of the others and witnesses to us the truth of all things.*"[1]

Our words, our explanations, and our testimonies can and will help to enlighten others, but it is the Holy Ghost who confirms those truths in the hearts of those we teach. This seems to be especially true when missionaries preach and testify to their investigators about the gospel. This confirming witness can come into the heart even when a person is not directly seeking truth or is not what we would think of as "ready" for the gospel. Here are two examples from the lives of missionaries that illustrate the power of the Holy Spirit's confirming witness of the truth.

> *Almost everyone has felt the influence of the Holy Ghost at some point in life. It is through the Holy Ghost that truth is confirmed upon our souls. But the special ministry of the Holy Ghost is to help people believe and follow the teachings of the Father and the Son.*
>
> M. RUSSELL BALLARD,
> *OUR SEARCH FOR HAPPINESS,* 84

Testify!

Two missionaries were tracting in a small town one afternoon. At one home, a middle-aged woman opened the door. She immediately recognized them for who they were and invited them in, though her manner seemed somewhat cool and curt. As they came into the living room, the husband, who had come out to shake their hands, quickly excused himself and went into the next room. As they thought about it later, one elder said it was as if the husband knew what was coming and wanted no part of it.

When the missionaries started to explain that they were called to share a message about Jesus Christ, the woman rudely interrupted them. She said she knew all about Mormon missionaries and their message. She had invited them in only in the hopes of saving their souls from hell. And then she launched into a tirade of criticism, accusations, and condemnation. She was loud, aggressive, combative, and insulting. Every time the missionaries tried to respond to her comments, she would cut them off, ridiculing them, telling them they were doomed to hell and that they were doing the work of the devil. This went on for about fifteen minutes without any letup. The senior companion reported what happened next:

"As I sat there, feeling more and more awful about what was happening, there came into my mind a single word: 'Testify!' When she finally paused to catch her breath, I jumped to my feet. Quietly but firmly I said the following: 'Mrs. Jones, we have listened to all you have to say. You are clearly convinced that we are not only wrong but evil. And it is your right to feel that way. Clearly, you are rejecting our message. But I testify to you in the name of the God whom we serve that the message we bring to you this day is true. I also testify to you that someday you and I shall meet again at the judgment bar of God. Then you will know for yourself, without the slightest shadow of doubt, that our message is true.'

"What happened next was astonishing," he went on. "For the first time since we had entered her home, she was totally speechless. She gaped at me when I sat down again. It was like she wanted to say something, but couldn't get it out. I felt strongly that there was nothing more to say, so we excused ourselves and left. Other than our brief farewell, not another word was spoken between us. But I came away that day with a testimony of the power of testimony."

This woman's heart was filled with anger and contention; one would hardly say that she was "touched by the Spirit." Yet something in that missionary's testimony brought the Spirit into the conversation in such a way that she was struck with great force and cut off the tirade. Was she edified? Maybe not in the usual sense of the word, but who knows for sure? This much is clear, however: The missionary and his companion were certainly blessed and edified by the Spirit that day.

This Is Really True!

The second example comes from my own experience. I had been in the mission field about five or six months and was serving as senior companion at that time. We were laboring in the town of Glasgow, in northeastern Montana. One member of the Glasgow Branch owned a huge wheat farm about twenty miles north of town. It was pretty isolated country.

One day after sacrament meeting, this rancher pulled me and my companion aside. He told us that he and his wife had been talking to his ranch foreman and his wife about the Church and that they were interested. He invited us to come up for dinner during the next week and give them the first discussion afterward. We, of course, immediately agreed.

When we arrived a few days later, the foreman and his wife

were very friendly and open as we had dinner together. It was clear that they were definitely receptive, which made the teaching setting after dinner nearly ideal.

Before describing what happened that evening, let me first say this about my testimony. I grew up in a gospel-centered family. My parents taught us throughout our childhood that God lives, that Jesus Christ is our Savior and Redeemer, and that Joseph Smith was a true prophet who restored the gospel to the earth. So I was a believer. I don't ever remember doubting any of what they said. When it came to Joseph Smith, I accepted it without question. I realize now that I had a testimony of him and his calling as prophet before I ever went into the mission field.

Now back to that night on a wheat farm in northern Montana. At this time, we had a set of missionary discussions that we were asked to memorize so that when it came time to give them, we would be freed up to adapt them to specific individual needs with confidence and ease. The first of these seven discussions centered on the Apostasy and Restoration. As part of the lesson we were asked to read the Joseph Smith story from the Pearl of Great Price and then talk about the Restoration.

As a companionship, we took turns teaching different parts of the lesson. As it happened, when it came time to read the Joseph Smith story, the teaching came back to me. As I opened

> *As I pray for the guidance of the Spirit, and seek to rise to the responsibility which has been given me, I don't ask for any special endowment. I ask only to go where the Lord would have me go, and only to receive what the Lord would have me receive, knowing that more important than sight is the witness that one may have by the witness of the Holy Ghost to his soul.*
>
> HAROLD B. LEE,
> *TEACHINGS*, 636

the scriptures and began to read from Joseph's own words, I could see that the couple were very attentive and receptive to what they were hearing. But then, suddenly, something totally unexpected happened. I came to the part where Joseph left his home on that beautiful spring morning and went into a grove of trees nearby. As I read about the Father and Son appearing to Joseph, there came this wonderful, intense clarity into my mind. It didn't come as words and it wasn't dramatic—not in the usual sense of the word. But suddenly I found that inside my mind the story was hitting me with great force. And I found myself saying to myself in my mind, even as I spoke, "This is true. This is *really* true."

If you were to ask me now when I got my testimony of Joseph Smith and the First Vision, I would tell you that I *learned* about him as a child, but I came to *know for myself* that he was a prophet of God one evening many years ago in northern Montana.

The couple were baptized a few weeks later. Sadly, I was transferred shortly thereafter and lost track of them. But to this day, when I read those words from section 50 of the Doctrine and Covenants about both teacher and learner being edified and rejoicing together, my mind goes back to that night when the Holy Ghost testified to me that it was true.

The Holy Ghost Carries It unto the Heart

Before leaving our discussion on the Holy Ghost's role as Testifier, we need to briefly note one important aspect of this witnessing function. In the closing chapter of his record, Nephi made this interesting observation about the Holy Ghost: "When a man speaketh by the power of the Holy Ghost the power of the Holy Ghost carrieth it *unto* the hearts of the children of men" (2 Nephi 33:1).

Note that he says *unto* and not *into*. This tiny difference in the preposition reminds us of a profound truth taught in one of our hymns:

> *He'll call, persuade, direct aright,*
> *And bless with wisdom, love, and light,*
> *In nameless ways be good and kind,*
> *But never force the human mind.*[2]

One of the greatest acts of agency is the willingness to open our hearts to the promptings of the Spirit. These are most often quiet, almost imperceptible whisperings. If we choose to open our hearts to the Spirit, the Holy Ghost can and will share His gifts and fulfill His functions with us. If, however, we choose to close our hearts to such promptings, then the Spirit withdraws. Alma taught this very clearly:

> He that will harden his heart, the same receiveth the lesser portion of the word; and he that will not harden his heart, to him is given the greater portion of the word, until it is given unto him to know the mysteries of God until he know them in full. And they that will harden their hearts, to them is given the lesser portion of the word until they know nothing concerning his mysteries. . . . Then if our hearts have been hardened, yea, if we have hardened our hearts against the word, insomuch that it has not been found in us, then will our state be awful, for then we shall be condemned. (Alma 12:10–11, 13)

One of the primary functions of the Holy Ghost is to testify of the Father and the Son and of the truth of the gospel. But if that is to happen in the teaching and learning setting, there is a responsibility for both the teacher and the learner to open their hearts so the Spirit can fulfill His function to teach and testify.

We must ever remember that agency is so sacred that Heavenly Father will never force the human heart, even with all His infinite power. And therefore, neither will the Spirit. Man may try to do so, but God does not. To put it another way, God allows us to be the guardians, or the gatekeepers, of our own hearts. We must, of our own free will, open our hearts to the Spirit, for even though He has a primary role to teach, He will not force Himself upon us. To do so would be contrary to the order of heaven. But when we do open our hearts, then He can testify and teach with power to us. Then faith is strengthened and testimony deepened. And that is what teaching by the Spirit is all about.

Please notice how the power of the Spirit carries the message unto but not necessarily into the heart. A teacher can explain, demonstrate, persuade, and testify, and do so with great spiritual power and effectiveness. Ultimately, however, the content of a message and the witness of the Holy Ghost penetrate into the heart only if a receiver allows them to enter.

DAVID A. BEDNAR,
"Seek Learning by Faith," 1

CHAPTER 6

THE HOLY GHOST BESTOWS THE GIFTS OF THE SPIRIT

—+>•⁙+—

PART I

After baptism, we are confirmed members of The Church of Jesus Christ of Latter-day Saints by the laying on of hands. After that, we are given the gift of the Holy Ghost. The actual wording is, "Receive the Holy Ghost." This is a reminder to us that this gift, which is beyond our ability to describe, is not automatically ours. We must take action to make the gift our own.

But the scriptures also speak of the *gifts*—plural—of the Spirit. This shouldn't be confusing. We are given the *gift* of the Holy Ghost. After that, the Holy Ghost can give us the *gifts* that are His to give. This is surely another very important function of the Holy Ghost, and many of those gifts directly bless our teaching efforts. So let us examine some of these gifts in greater detail.

FUNCTION 3: THE HOLY GHOST BESTOWS THE GIFTS OF THE SPIRIT

It would seem like an obvious truth that the bestowal of the gifts of the Spirit would be a direct and important part of our efforts to teach the gospel, both informally and formally. But I must admit that for many years in my career as a religious educator, I hadn't really thought much about the gifts of the Spirit and the part they play in our teaching. Perhaps that was because back then, when I thought of teaching by the Spirit, I was thinking primarily of formal classroom experiences, particularly in my own seminary and institute classes. Now I understand that those gifts are not just wonderful blessings given to individuals. They are frequently—even constantly—bestowed during the process of teaching and preaching as well.

There are three places in scripture in which the gifts of the Spirit are specifically listed, but as Elder Bruce R. McConkie pointed out, other gifts of the Spirit are mentioned throughout the scriptures. He also noted that since the Holy Ghost is an infinite, divine Being, His gifts are also infinite:

> From the writings of Paul (1 Cor. 12; 13; 14), and of Moroni (Moro. 10), and from the revelations received by Joseph Smith (D&C 46), we gain a clear knowledge of spiritual gifts and how they operate. . . . *These are by no means all of the gifts. In the fullest sense, they are infinite in number and endless in their manifestations.*[1]

It would take a very large book to fully discuss all of these gifts and the role they play in teaching by the Spirit. Therefore, we shall select only a few of the gifts to discuss here and in the chapters that follow.

The Gift of Discernment

In section 46 of the Doctrine and Covenants, we find the most extensive list of the gifts of the Spirit. There we find the concept of discernment mentioned twice: "To others [is given] the *discerning* of spirits" (v. 23). Then the Lord adds this: "And unto the bishop of the church, and unto such as God shall appoint and ordain to watch over the church and to be elders unto the church, are to have it given unto them *to discern all those gifts* lest there shall be any among you professing and yet be not of God" (v. 27).

Discernment is the ability to perceive, understand, discriminate, or distinguish something from its surroundings or its context. It also means to have an acute sensitivity to things and an unusually wise sense of judgment. It implies an ability that is not commonly found in most people.

In the scriptures, the idea of discernment often describes one person's ability to discern or know the thoughts and feelings of another. Here are just a few examples:

- One several occasions as He was teaching the people, Jesus confounded them with His answers because He knew their thoughts (see Matthew 9:4; 12:25; Luke 11:17).
- In his great call to repentance given to his people, Jacob said that "by the help of the all-powerful Creator of heaven and earth I can tell you concerning your thoughts" (Jacob 2:5).
- When the Zoramites were trying to entrap Amulek with promises of bribery, Amulek did "know of their designs" and "perceived their thoughts" (Alma 10:17).
- Zeezrom was a leader in the attempt to discredit Amulek. When Amulek confounded him, Alma said to Zeezrom, "Thou seest that thy thoughts are made known unto us by his Spirit" (Alma 12:3).
- After his stunning defeat of the enemies of King Lamoni at the waters of Sebus, Ammon was called into the presence of the king. Lamoni was speechless with fear and didn't respond. But Ammon "perceived the thoughts of the king" and guessed why he was unable to speak. This amazed

Lamoni even more because "he beheld that Ammon could discern his thoughts" (Alma 18:16, 18).

In each of these cases, we see how the gift of discernment had a direct impact on the teaching experience.

The Mind Scanner

Most of us have had the annoying—or sometimes downright unpleasant—experience of passing through a security scanner in an airport, a department store, or a courtroom. These are designed to detect anything we are carrying that might prove to be a security threat to those inside.

One day many years ago, as I watched my students file into my seminary class, the idea of a scanner crossed my mind. As I watched their faces and their body language and wondered what was going on inside their minds, I had this thought: Wouldn't it be great if someone invented *a mind scanner* that could read the mental, emotional, and spiritual state of our . . . [fill in the blank here: students, children, spouses, ward members, bosses, business associates, friends].

I began imagining what kinds of things I might find on the printout from such a scanner. Things like:

- Had a bitter fight with her mother just before leaving for school. Didn't have time to wash her hair and it's a mess. Very foul mood. Half spoiling for a verbal fight.
- Just found out he's replacing the starting quarterback this afternoon. Very happy, but also pretty cocky and experiencing a lot of pride right now.
- Didn't sleep well, tired, irritable. Wants people to leave her alone.
- Got an answer to a problem he's been struggling with for

weeks during his personal scripture study. Thrilled and joyful to know that God knows and loves him.

- Feels totally lost and alone. Is convinced he's weird, a geek, a zero. Though he has not seriously considered taking his life, he often wonders if life will ever change for him. He despairs because the answer always comes back no.
- Found out last night that her father has terminal cancer and has less than six months to live.
- Is a happy, well-adjusted, and confident student. Feels life is good and is basically happy all the time. She loves seminary, likes you as a teacher, and has come eager and ready to learn.
- That "harmless" little joke you made about her in class yesterday deeply hurt her. She has vowed never to answer another question and plans to go to the principal later today and ask for a transfer out of your class.

I thought of other places these mind scanners might be useful. How might having a scanner at each of our children's bedroom doors change how we interacted with them? Spouses might set one up at the entrance to the home so they could get a reading as the other partner came home from work or shopping. Putting one at each of the chapel doors before sacrament meeting might overwhelm the bishop. He might have to program the machine to beep or set off a flashing red light that signaled only the most urgent of problems coming through.

While amusing and intriguing, I think most of us would agree that using such a scanner would not be wise. It would be too invasive of personal privacy. And talk about information overload! A teacher or parent could easily become paralyzed with knowing that much about another person.

Then, as my mind played with this idea, another thought came. Isn't that one of the functions of the Holy Ghost as He teaches us? Not to tell us every thought of someone else, of course, but to alert us to real problems going on in those we work with, to help us sense their thoughts and feelings and enlighten us on what to do about them? That is one of His functions: to help us discern key thoughts and feelings when the need is there.

The Doctor and the Seminary Teacher

Early in my career as a seminary teacher, my supervisor shared this experience in an in-service training session. He had recently taken his daughter to a doctor who was a fellow ward member and a good friend. At the conclusion of the examination, the father received a twenty-seven-dollar invoice for the office call. (You can tell this was a long time ago.)

The next Sunday, the supervisor couldn't resist heckling his MD friend a little. "I find this interesting," he began. "I brought my daughter to your office. You took her to the examination room where you interviewed her one-on-one about her illness. She told you her symptoms. You asked for more details, which she gave willingly. You then made a diagnosis and prescribed treatment. In all, you took about ten minutes with her. And for that you charged me twenty-seven dollars. If you see four patients an hour on the average, that's better than a hundred dollars an hour that you make.

"But five times every week, your daughter comes to my seminary class for nearly an hour. She comes with thirty-two others. Most of these students are not only *not* willing to tell me what their problems are and what symptoms they are having, but in many cases they are actually trying to hide them from me. Yet I am expected to simultaneously examine them, diagnose their problems, then decide what 'treatment' they need and try to give it to them before the hour is over. And," he concluded ruefully, "I don't make anywhere near a hundred dollars an hour."

After chuckling over the memory of his experience for a

moment, the supervisor then said, "But after saying that, I realized that I have something that makes it all right. I have the right to have the Spirit present in the classroom, and the Spirit can do all of that and do it perfectly."

Discernment in Our Callings

Speaking of the gift of discernment mentioned in D&C 46:27, President Stephen L Richards gave this valuable insight:

> I believe that this gift when highly developed arises largely out of an acute sensitivity to impressions—spiritual impressions, if you will—to read under the surface as it were, to detect hidden evil, and *more importantly to find the good that may be concealed. The highest type of discernment is that which perceives in others and uncovers for them their better natures, the good inherent within them.*[2]

Sister Ardeth G. Kapp, who served as general president of the Young Women from 1984 to 1992, shared a wonderful example of how this ability to see the potential good in someone else actually works:

> It was in a second grade elementary classroom. The student-teacher held the children captive with her story-telling skills. In great detail she told of a cross old man whose name was Mr. Black. In contrast, the account was given in similar detail of a Mr. Brown who was kind and thoughtful and loved by everyone. At the conclusion of the story, the teacher asked the children, "How many of you would like to be a neighbor to Mr. Brown?" Every hand was raised high. Then almost as an afterthought, she inquired if there was anyone who would like to have Mr. Black for a neighbor.

A little boy in a faded green shirt near the back of the room began to raise his hand, which brought a ripple of quiet amusement from the children. Hesitating only briefly, he looked around at his friends and still mustered the courage to hold his hand high and to stand alone in his difference. When called on for an explanation to his single vote, he spoke in a soft tone. "Well," he said, "I'd like Mr. Black to be my neighbor, because if he was, my mom would make a cake for me to take to him, and then he wouldn't be that way anymore." A hush fell over the room. Everyone felt something wonderful that they couldn't explain. A little child broke the silence like a benediction: "Oh, I wish I'd said that."[3]

First, . . . discernment helps us detect hidden error and evil in others. Second, and more important, it helps us detect hidden errors and evil in ourselves. Thus the spiritual gift of discernment is not exclusively about discerning other people and situations, but . . . is also about discerning things as they really are within us. Third, it helps us find and bring forth the good that may be concealed in us. Oh, what a blessing and a source of protection and direction is the spiritual gift of discernment!

David A. Bednar,
"Quick to Observe," 35

Here is an example of how this gift can work outside of a formal teaching setting.

"Get Him to the Temple"

A friend shared with me the following experience he had while serving as a bishop. He had in his ward an older man who had been excommunicated for adultery many years before. This man faithfully attended his meetings, volunteered regularly for welfare and other service assignments, treated his wife with dignity and respect, and was otherwise exemplary in his conduct. But he did not hold a temple recommend and had not, as nearly as the bishop could determine, since he had been excommunicated some twenty years before, even though he had been rebaptized about five years later.

So, one day, the bishop called him in and interviewed him. He noted that the man didn't hold a temple recommend but that, as far as the bishop could ascertain, he was worthy to have one. He paid his tithing, lived the Word of Wisdom, and so on. The man agreed, saying that he was doing all of those things, but that because of some things that had happened in the past, he didn't feel like he was worthy to go to the temple. Feeling that he needed to push the man a little, the bishop asked if he would mind sharing what had happened. Here is the story he told.

Within a year of his marriage in the temple, he learned that his wife had been having an affair with another man for many months. Now she wanted a divorce so she could marry this man. He was absolutely crushed. Bitter, heartbroken, angry, and frustrated, he emotionally withdrew into a shell. One day a month or so later, as he was talking with a female associate at work, she asked him why he had been so down lately. That did it. It all came out as he unburdened himself. She was not a member of the Church and reacted with understanding and sympathy. They began having long talks and going to lunch with each other. One night he took her home, and she invited him in. One thing led to another, and, with her full encouragement, they eventually went to bed together. The next morning he was shattered by what he had done. He immediately went to his bishop and confessed. A short time later, he was excommunicated.

When he finished telling the bishop his story, his head was down and his voice was low. The bishop asked if there had been any other moral transgressions since that time. There had been none. Then the bishop said, "As I looked into his face and saw the sorrow and heartache there, I had this strong impression come to me. In my mind it was almost like a voice, only it was more of a feeling. It said to me, 'This is a good and worthy man. He has fully repented. He has suffered enough. *Get him to the temple.*'"

The bishop reported that it took some persuading, but that night this good brother agreed to be interviewed for a temple recommend. The bishop sent him right over to the stake presidency to get it signed by them as well. From that point on, this faithful member attended the temple at least once a week. After about a year, he was called as a temple worker and served as such for nearly five more years before he died.

How I love that concept taught by President Richards: "The highest type of discernment is that which perceives in others and uncovers for them their better natures, the good inherent within them."

CHAPTER 7

THE HOLY GHOST BESTOWS
THE GIFTS OF THE SPIRIT

———+>•<+———

PART II

In chapter 4, we defined teaching by the Spirit in this way:

> *Teaching by the Spirit takes place when the Holy Ghost is fulfilling His role and His functions with either the teacher or the learner or both.*

We then said that to better understand what this means, we needed to discuss those functions in detail. In this chapter, we shall continue our discussion of *Function 3: The Holy Ghost Bestows the Gifts of the Spirit.* We shall do so by looking at some of the other gifts of the Spirit.

"To Others It Is Given to Believe on Their Words"

One of the gifts of the Spirit listed in section 46 of the Doctrine and Covenants is what we think of as a testimony, though that word is not used in the passage itself. It says, "To some it is given by the Holy Ghost to *know* that Jesus Christ is the Son of God, and that he was crucified for the sins of the world" (v. 13).

That kind of a sure testimony is a wonderful gift that is critical to our movement toward eternal life.

But what immediately follows in the next verse describes a related gift. Though some might say this is a lesser gift, the end result is the same. The Lord says, "To others it is given to *believe* on their words, that they also might have eternal life if they continue faithful" (v. 14).

This too is a gift of testimony, but of a different nature. The first suggests an assurance one has from his or her own knowledge. The second is another gift given to those who, for whatever reason, do not know the gospel truths with that same surety. But the Spirit blesses them with an ability to trust in someone else's testimony sufficiently to keep them believing until they get their own sure knowledge. Young children would be a common example of those who are given this gift. New converts would be as well.

"Because My Mother Read It"

I remember an experience from my mission that illustrates this gift. I was the trainer for a new elder who had been in the field for only a few weeks. He was a young man I would describe as "gentle of soul." His desire to serve was simple and pure.

One day as we were tracting, we came to the home of an evangelical preacher. He knew who we were and invited us in with obvious relish—kind of like a lion inviting an impala into his den. Immediately he began to rail on us. He scoffed at us, mocked our answers, and treated us with open scorn.

When my companion tried to answer one of his questions using the Book of Mormon, this man cut him off sharply. "So," he sneered, "have you read the Book of Mormon all the way through?"

My companion's head dropped. "No, not yet."

The pastor literally shouted at him, "If you haven't even read it, then how can you say that it's true?"

That was a good question, and I was frantically trying to decide whether to jump in and attempt to rescue my companion, but before I could do so, his head came up and he said this: "My mother has read the Book of Mormon many times, and she's told me that she knows that it's true. And I know that my mother would never lie to me."

The pastor was disgusted. He shook his head in disgust at such "naivete," muttering about the impossibility of knowing a book was true if you hadn't read it. We left shortly thereafter, feeling whipped and discouraged. But later, the more I thought about it, the more I decided that although my companion's testimony might have seemed weak in the eyes of the world, it was sweet and pure and true. Now I realize it was a wonderful example of this gift of the Spirit that allows us to believe on the testimony of others. I suppose that if I had asked my companion afterward if he thought he had taught with the Spirit that day, he would probably have said no. But he would be wrong. If nothing else, I know that I was taught by the Spirit that day.

He Never Knew

One Church member shared this experience with his bishop. He said that in his seminary years he had been through a rough time. His parents were in the midst of a divorce. He had taken up with some questionable friends, and he was generally angry at the world. But his mother insisted that he go to seminary or lose his car privileges. "So I went," he said, "but I gave my teacher fits. And when I wasn't doing that, I sat in the back of the class with my head down, daring him to try to teach me.

"But I listened at times, in spite of myself. When he taught about the Savior, I was skeptical. I tried to push it away. But one thing was absolutely certain. I knew *that he knew* Jesus was the Christ. After I graduated, I started to realize where my life was taking me. I remember one day wanting to come back. As I wondered how to start on the road back, I suddenly thought of my teacher and his testimony. I decided that if he knew, then I could know too. I started reading the Book of Mormon and praying. The rest is history. I did come back. I served a mission, married in the temple, and have been active ever since. Much of that was because of that man's testimony. I would guess that if you brought up my name with that teacher, he would probably never remember me. If he did, he would likely believe that he had failed with me. What would he say if he knew that it was his testimony that touched my heart somehow, even though *he never knew* that it did?"

The Gift of Knowledge and Wisdom

I shall use my own father to illustrate the two gifts of knowledge and wisdom, which are listed separately but are closely related (see D&C 46:17–18). My father was very intelligent. He was born and raised in the very small town of Fountain Green in central Utah. He graduated from high school with excellent grades. From one of my uncles, I learned after Dad's death that he had once solved a calculus problem in the high school math book that even the calculus teacher couldn't solve.

After graduation, Dad was accepted at the University of Utah and went north to start his studies in September 1929. About a month later, on October 29, 1929, the stock market went into a free fall, taking America into the Great Depression. My father was forced to drop out of the university and find a job. Life was such that he was never able to go back. As a result, he spent most of his life as a pipe fitter at the Kennecott Copper smelter in Magna, Utah. He always regretted his loss of that education and often mourned the fact that he was "an uneducated man." Perhaps that was so, but he never lost his love of learning and his desire for knowledge. And many times in my life I learned that he had a unique gift for wise counsel. The following story is one example of how he blessed my life with that gift.

Love Is a Living Thing

As the time drew close for my mission, I was seriously dating a girl. We had been dating long enough that we had talked about marriage. She was a beautiful and wonderful young woman, and we were very close. I loved her a great deal. Once the mission call came, however, a cruel reality began to settle in on my mind. I realized that there were going to be a lot of wolves prowling around while I was gone and that I would have no way to fend them off. So I started thinking seriously about formally asking her to wait for me. And by *formally asking,* I meant putting an engagement ring on her finger.

But another part of me was reluctant to tie her down. I knew that two years was a long time for an attractive young woman to stay away from the dating and courting scene. I was quite troubled about what to do. So one day, I went out to the barn where Dad was working and asked if I could talk to him. He put aside his work, and we sat down. I explained to him my dilemma, then put it straight to him: "Should I give her an engagement ring and ask her to wait for me or not?"

He thought about it for a long moment; then he said this: "Well, you'll have to make that choice for yourself, but remember this: love is a living thing."

I gave him a puzzled look. "What's that supposed to mean?"

He sat back. "It means that love is not a piece of granite that you set up on a shelf for two years, then take back down when you return home and find it just the same. Love is a living thing. And living things require constant nourishment, or they wither away. Living things can be hurt and damaged, even to the point where they die. Living things are either growing or dying. And that's true of love, too."

I think I just stared at him. That was so unlike my father. I don't think he ever talked much about love or dating or courtship. When I pushed him for a more definitive answer, he said it again. "As you make your decision, just keep that in mind. Love is a living thing."

I did keep it in mind, actually. I thought about it a lot over the next few days. And I finally decided not to ask her for any commitments. "I hope you're still here when I get back," I told her, "but I want you to be free to date if you choose."

She *was* there when I returned. And Dad proved to be right. She was still a wonderful woman. She had grown and matured tremendously in those two years, as had I. But things had changed between us, and after dating two or three times we agreed that it wasn't going to work and went our separate ways. It was a painful moment for both of us—but how grateful I was that there wasn't an engagement ring to further complicate things!

That wasn't the end of Dad's influence. I don't know how many times his words have come back to me over the years. When my wife and I were having differences that were pulling us apart, I would hear those words again: "Love is a living thing." I have shared that concept with many others over the years, in counseling sessions, in classes and workshops, and even to a couple of young missionaries wondering if they should give their girlfriends an engagement ring before they left on their missions.

I thank God for my father's gift of wisdom, for I was edified that day, and that made a huge difference in my life.

CHAPTER 8

THE HOLY GHOST BESTOWS
THE GIFTS OF THE SPIRIT

—+>•<+—

PART III

SOME SPIRITUAL GIFTS WE MAY NOT NORMALLY ASSOCIATE WITH TEACHING BY THE SPIRIT

Some of the gifts of the Spirit may not, at first, seem to have a direct association with teaching or preaching. It is not that they are of lesser value, only that they seem to be gifts given to individuals in nonteaching settings.

The gift of tongues is one of those that comes immediately to mind. The gift of healing is another. Other examples would be the gift "to know the differences of administration" and "to know the diversities of operations" (D&C 46:15–16). These latter two, in my mind, seemed to be more related to leadership functions than to teaching. This was back in those early years when I thought of teaching only in terms of formal classroom settings. Now I understand that "teaching" is a major function of leadership. So it is appropriate that we discuss these other gifts here so as to broaden our view of how the Holy Ghost functions in teaching.

The Gift of Tongues

By its very nature, the gift of what we call "speaking in tongues" can be more dramatic than the other gifts because it is so outwardly visible. When someone stands up and speaks to a group in a language that he or she does not know, or when others hear and understand a language other than their own, that is pretty sensational. Because of that, some people may be tempted to view the gift of tongues as more important than other gifts. And unfortunately, it is a gift that can be counterfeited. If people start to speak in what they claim is another tongue but what is, in reality, simply meaningless babble, who's to say whether that is real or not?

The Apostle Paul spent a whole chapter in an epistle to the Corinthian Saints cautioning them about elevating the gift of tongues above other gifts. He also said that if the gift was manifest, it should be accompanied by the gift of the interpretation of tongues so as to validate and give meaning to the gift (see 1 Corinthians 14). In other words, this gift is real and valuable, but it comes with cautions.

There are only two gifts that [are] made visible—the gift of tongues and the gift of prophecy. These are things that are the most talked about, and yet if a person spoke in an unknown tongue, according to Paul's testimony, he would be a barbarian to those present. They would say that it was gibberish; and if he prophesied they would call it nonsense. The gift of tongues is the smallest gift perhaps of the whole, and yet it is one that is the most sought after.

JOSEPH SMITH,
Teachings, 246

The corrupting of the gift of tongues also happened early in the history of the Church. It reached the point where the Prophet Joseph Smith warned the Saints about it on several occasions. "Satan will no doubt trouble you about the gift of tongues," he said as early as 1833.[1] Later, when missionaries started coming back with all kinds of stories of false spirits they had encountered, Joseph further explained:

> Not every spirit, or vision, or singing, is of God. . . . Speak not in the gift of tongues without understanding it, or without interpretation. The devil can speak in tongues; the adversary will come with his work; he can tempt all classes; can speak in English or Dutch. Let no one speak in tongues unless he interpret, except by the consent of the one who is placed to preside; then he may discern or interpret, or another may.[2]

Clearly, we are not suggesting that teachers should be seeking for opportunities to speak in tongues to their students in classroom settings, or that they should give priesthood blessings to the sick and afflicted in their classrooms. On the other hand, it would be shortsighted to pass over these gifts without linking them to teaching by the Spirit.

THE INTERPRETATION OF LANGUAGES

As noted earlier, the gifts of the Spirit are listed in three places—1 Corinthians 12, Moroni 10, and section 46 of the Doctrine and Covenants. A careful comparison of how these three sources refer to the gift of tongues is instructive. Paul called the gift "divers kinds of tongues" and "the interpretation of tongues" (1 Corinthians 12:10). Moroni described it as "all kinds of tongues" and "the interpretation of languages and of divers kinds of tongues" (Moroni 10:15–16). And the Doctrine and Covenants calls it "the interpretation of tongues" (D&C 46:25). The phrase *interpretation of languages* suggests that there is more to this gift than just speaking to a group in a language we do not normally speak.

It Is Not Possible

A colleague of mine in the Church Educational System shared this experience with me many years ago. His responsibilities at that time included the supervision of our programs in Asia. On one occasion he was in Taiwan, having lunch in the hotel where he was staying. Another American came up and asked if he could join him.

As it turned out, that man was in Taiwan as a representative of one of the mainstream Christian churches. He and his wife had been sent to Taiwan to learn Mandarin Chinese prior to their being assigned to do missionary work among the Chinese people. When my associate asked him if he was engaged in that missionary work now, he explained that they had not yet started formal missionary service, but soon would begin. How long had they been here? my associate asked. "Almost two years," was the reply.

My associate was quite taken aback. He explained that he too belonged to a church that sent missionaries out into the world to teach the gospel, including to the Chinese people. But when he explained that our missionaries come out after only a couple of months of language training and are put right into teaching situations, the man openly scoffed. That couldn't be, especially with a language as difficult as Chinese, which took literally years of study. By "coincidence," just then two of our full-time missionaries came into the hotel to meet someone. My friend saw them and called them over. After introducing them to his lunch companion, he asked them how long they had been in Taiwan. One said four months, the other said seven or eight. "Talk to my friend here in Mandarin," he suggested. "He's studying the language too."

As they began to converse, the man's astonishment grew more

and more evident. "You cannot be telling the truth about how long you have been here," he finally said. "It is not possible that you have been here for so short a time. It simply is not possible."

Missionaries and Foreign Languages

We see this quiet miracle happening with tens of thousands of young men and women all around the world. Doesn't that also represent one aspect of the gift of tongues? And when they speak with that remarkable ability, or when their investigators are able to get past their halting, stumbling "murder" of the native language and still be touched by the Spirit, aren't these manifestations of teaching and preaching by the Spirit?

I have a granddaughter currently serving a mission in Japan. Japanese is another very difficult language. During that time when she was still feeling very limited and inadequate in her ability to converse in Japanese, one day she and her companion were teaching an investigator. When it was her turn to teach, she found herself trying to explain a gospel principle that was beyond her language capacity. But suddenly she realized that she was speaking clearly and fluently. The investigator was understanding. She could see that in her eyes. When the lesson was over, she was back to struggling, but for that moment, she had what I believe Moroni meant by "the gift of languages."

As another example, while my wife and I were serving in the Europe West Area Presidency, we saw numerous instances of this gift, not just with the missionaries but with our mission presidents and their wives as well. We saw their children acquire the languages of the countries where they were serving with remarkable speed and facility. One of our presidents had served a French-speaking mission himself and was called to preside over the Belgium Brussels Mission. Belgium is primarily a French-speaking country, but the mission also included Holland, where Dutch is spoken. In a way, it was as if he were in charge of two separate missions. He determined that he could not fully serve the Dutch people and his Dutch-speaking missionaries if he could only speak French and English. Shortly after arriving, he decided he had to learn Dutch. In a matter of a few months, and with very little formal training, he was able to converse and even teach in Dutch when he spoke in meetings.

These are less dramatic but still quite remarkable examples of how the Spirit bestows the gift of tongues in what is clearly teaching by the Spirit. But the other, more dramatic experiences happen too, though much less frequently. Here are two examples of remarkable manifestations of that gift that occurred in formal teaching settings, though not a traditional classroom.

The Day of Pentecost

One of the great teaching moments found in scripture happened just two months following the death and Resurrection of the Savior. The Twelve were in Jerusalem. It was the time of the Jewish festival called the Feast of Weeks (in Hebrew, *Shavuot*). In the New Testament, it is called the Day of Pentecost.

This was an important feast day, and Jewish people from all over the Roman Empire had come to Jerusalem to celebrate. Many of them had never lived in the Holy Land and didn't speak Aramaic, a local form of Hebrew. The Twelve were out among the people teaching. A large group gathered to hear them.

What followed began with something very dramatic. There was the sound "as of a rushing mighty wind," and then tongues of fire appeared and "sat upon each of them." The Apostles were filled with the Spirit and "began to speak *with other tongues,* as the Spirit gave them utterance" (Acts 2:3–4). The people were astonished, of course. They cried out, "Behold, are not all these which

When I sat in school a student as you, I wondered about the reality of the gift of tongues and the interpretation of tongues. I did not doubt it because it was part of the Church, but I wondered. Tonight I want to bear you witness that the interpretation of tongues is a reality. I witnessed it in New Zealand . . . in 1921; again in Aintab [Turkey] when President J. Wilford Booth was interpreting in the Turkish language what I was speaking in English; and a third experience in Holland—when President Zappey was interpreter.

DAVID O. MCKAY,
STEPPING STONES TO AN ABUNDANT LIFE, 243–44

speak Galilaeans? And how hear we every man in our own tongue, wherein we were born?" (vv. 7–8).

This is astonishing. It wasn't just Peter or John who spoke in a different tongue. All of the Apostles did, and, evidently, they spoke in multiple languages. Remember what we previously read about the result of teaching by the Spirit? "He that preacheth and he that receiveth, understand one another, and both are edified and rejoice together" (D&C 50:22). What better description could there be of what happened that day?

We are not told how many were in the multitude at Pentecost, but we are told this: "They were pricked in their heart, and said unto Peter and to the rest of the apostles, Men and brethren, what shall we do?" Peter's answer was simple: Repent and be baptized so you can have the Holy Ghost as well (see Acts 2:37–38). *Three thousand of them*—the equivalent of a full stake today—gladly did just that and joined the Church *that day!* (see Acts 2:41).

An Apostle Speaks and the People Hear

In the quote by President McKay found in the text box above, he made reference to an experience he had in New Zealand in

1921. In this case, this was not the gift of speaking in tongues but rather the gift of the interpretation of tongues. Here is his account:

> One of the most important events on my world tour of the missions of the Church was the gift of interpretation of the English tongue to the Saints of New Zealand, at a session of their conference, held on the 23rd day of April, 1921. . . . When I looked over that vast assemblage and contemplated the great expectations that filled the hearts of all who had met together, I realized how inadequately I might satisfy the ardent desires of their souls, and I yearned, most earnestly, for the gift of tongues that I might be able to speak to them in their native language.
>
> Until that moment I had not given much serious thought to the gift of tongues, but on that occasion, I wished with all my heart, that I might be worthy of that divine power. . . . I faced an audience that had assembled with unusual expectations, and I then realized, as never before, the great responsibility of my office. From the depth of my soul, I prayed for divine assistance.
>
> When I arose to give my address, I said to Brother Stuart Meha, our interpreter, that I would speak without his translating, sentence by sentence what I said, and then to the audience I continued: "I wish, oh, how I wish I had the power to speak to you in your own tongue, that I might tell you what is in my heart; but since I have not the gift, I pray, and I ask you to pray, that you might have the spirit of interpretation, of discernment, that you may understand at least the spirit while I am speaking, and then you will get the words and the thought when Brother Meha interprets."
>
> My sermon lasted forty minutes, and I have never

addressed a more attentive, a more respectful audience. My listeners were in perfect rapport—this I knew when I saw tears in their eyes. Some of them at least, perhaps most of them, who did not understand English, had the gift of interpretation. Brother Sidney Christy, a native New Zealander, who had been a student at Brigham Young University, at the close of my address, whispered to me, "Brother McKay, they got your message!" "Yes," I replied, "I think so, but for the benefit of some who may not have understood, we shall have Brother Meha give a synopsis of it in Maori."

During the translation, *some of the Maoris corrected him on some points,* showing that they had a clear conception of what had been said in English.[3]

THE GIFT OF HEALING

As noted earlier, the gift of healing would rarely be found in a formal classroom setting, but that doesn't mean that when it does happen it has nothing to do with teaching.

"That's When I Knew There Is Real Power in the Priesthood"

A young man I know well shared this experience he had when he was about fourteen. He said he had received a call from his home teaching companion one night. This man explained that he had just received a request to come and help one of their assigned families. A daughter was very seriously ill. They asked if their home teacher could help the father give her a priesthood blessing. This wise home teacher could have gone alone, but he decided that he had a home teaching companion who needed to accompany him, even though he didn't hold the Melchizedek Priesthood and couldn't participate directly in the blessing.

When they got there, the girl was obviously very ill. She had a high fever and was drenched in perspiration. She was moaning and thrashing about. She hadn't been able to sleep and was totally exhausted. The young man stood back with others in the family as the home teacher anointed the girl. Then the father sealed the anointing and gave her a blessing. In the blessing, her father told her that her fever would soon break and that she would be able to sleep without pain.

When they were finished, they went back into the living room while the mother stayed with her daughter. The home teacher and companion visited for a few minutes with the family, then prepared to go. As they were about to leave, the mother came out to join them. The relief on her face was evident. "She's asleep," she said. "And her fever has broken. She's going to be all right."

By the time he got to this point in his narrative, this young man was quite emotional. In a choked voice he said, "It hadn't been more than five minutes before things changed. That's when I knew that there is real power in the priesthood."

On that night, the gift of healing also provided a significant teaching experience for a young boy of fourteen, as well as for his senior home teaching companion, a father and mother, and several brothers and sisters. I can't say for sure because I wasn't there, but I am guessing that not one of those involved in that experience thought of it as a "teaching by the Spirit" experience. But they were taught that night. I was taught later by that young man. And now, hopefully, you have been taught by the Spirit as well.

The Holy Ghost is a teacher. The gifts He offers to us bring remarkable blessings, but they also teach us. One of the functions of the Holy Ghost in teaching by the Spirit is the bestowal of the gifts of the Spirit.

CHAPTER 9

THE HOLY GHOST BESTOWS THE FRUITS OF THE SPIRIT

———→>•<←———

FUNCTION 4: THE HOLY GHOST BRINGS THE FRUITS OF THE SPIRIT

We have discussed the gifts of the Spirit, how they are evidence of the Holy Ghost's role as teacher, and how they relate to our call to teach the gospel by the Spirit. But in the New Testament we find a slightly different phrase. The Apostle Paul twice referred to what he called "the fruit of the Spirit"—a phrase not used by any of the other authors of scripture. In Galatians 5:22–23, Paul lists these fruits as "love, joy, peace, longsuffering, gentleness, goodness, faith." In Ephesians 5:9, he says, "For the fruit of the Spirit is in all goodness and righteousness and truth." Though he didn't use that exact phrase in his epistle to the Romans, we find the same general idea: "Now the God of hope fill you with all joy and peace in believing, that ye may abound in hope, through the power of the Holy Ghost" (Romans 15:13).

How are the *gifts* of the Spirit related to the *fruits* of the Spirit? Is this just a different way to say the same thing? I think not. The basic meaning of the word *gift* is something of value that is given to another. The common definition of *fruit* is a variety of different food products that come from plants. These usually are the result of relatively slow growth and development over a period of time called the growing season. By extension, fruit can also describe the results of some kind of meaningful human effort, as in, "He enjoyed the fruits of his labor."

Using those definitions, we could then say that the gifts of the Spirit are specific blessings bestowed by the Holy Ghost to help us as we strive to live the gospel. Many of these define abilities or skills that help us to live the gospel better—discernment, testimony, knowledge, wisdom, the gift of healing, the ability to speak in tongues. But the fruits of the Spirit seem more like character attributes, what we might call deep-seated virtues that become part of our nature. Like the fruit of the vine or the harvest of the orchard, these are the results of careful cultivation, pruning, and watchful care. Here is Paul's list of the fruits of the Spirit:

- Love
- Joy
- Peace
- Longsuffering
- Gentleness
- Goodness
- Faith

- Meekness
- Temperance
- Righteousness
- Truth
- Hope
- Believing

Obviously, "gifts" and "fruits" are not hard and fast categories. Wisdom, for example, is listed as a gift of the Spirit, but it feels more like a fruit of the Spirit. Faith is found in both lists. This close relationship between the two shouldn't be too surprising, since both come from the Spirit.

To put it another way, the gifts of the Spirit seem more closely related to *what* we teach (truth, the gospel, knowledge) and *how* we teach it (with testimony, clarity, knowledge, wisdom, discernment). But the fruits of the Spirit are the results of this teaching, or another *why* of our teaching. We teach by the Spirit so that people will be edified. One could almost say that these fruits of the Spirit become the "building blocks" of edification. These are what the building is made of.

While we cannot explore each of them, here are some examples of how the fruits of the Spirit indicate that teaching by the Spirit is taking or has taken place.

"I Couldn't Believe I Held My Tongue"

A mother describes an experience she had with a daughter of about sixteen. The teenager was being extremely rude and rebellious and saying things that deeply hurt her mother. "My first reaction," the mother reported, "was to strike back in anger, to hurt her like she was hurting me. I wanted to impose some punishment that would teach my daughter the consequences of her actions." But she did not. "I couldn't believe it," she said, "but I was able to hold my tongue that day. I just turned away and left without speaking." Later that night the daughter came and, in tears, apologized to her mother. She said that she had been going through a particularly rough day but now deeply regretted being so hurtful. Then the mother said this: "I was so grateful that I had been able to hold my tongue. What followed that night was a sweet and wonderful thing."

Two of the fruits of the Spirit are longsuffering (also known as patience) and temperance.

A Seminary Survey

A team of researchers were filming some "man-on-the-street" interviews of seminary students for a Church Educational System video. One question they asked was, "Tell us about your seminary experience. What is seminary like for you?" They expected to hear things like how much the students liked (or didn't like) their teachers, or how they enjoyed being with their friends, or about some of the fun activities they had in class. They got some of those responses, of course, but to their surprise what they heard again and again were statements like this:

- "I look forward to seminary because it's the one time every day when I can find a moment of peace."
- "Even if the rest of my day is going bad, seminary provides me a refuge from the world."
- "Seminary makes me feel good about myself."
- "Seminary makes me want to be a better person."
- "I almost always leave seminary happy."
- "On some days, I can't wait to leave the halls of my high school, where there is swearing and foul jokes, and walk across the parking lot to the seminary. It gives me the strength to get through the rest of the day."
- "My situation at home is pretty bad sometimes, but I can always count on seminary to get me through."

Some fruits of the Spirit are peace, goodness, joy, and hope.

"I Gave My Brother a Hug"

One young man, with a bit of wonder in his voice, made this comment to a friend: "In family home evening last night, we had a lesson about a Book of Mormon story. It had nothing to do with the family, and my father didn't really ask us to do anything special afterward. But as we finished, I looked at my younger brother. I don't know what came over me. We fight a lot. But suddenly I wanted to go over and give him a big hug. So I did."

One of the fruits of the Spirit is love.

"I Love It When You Pray"

A home teacher was assigned to a part-member family in his ward. The father was a former returned missionary and had been married in the temple, but he had been totally out of activity in the Church for many years. After a divorce, he married a woman who was not a member of the Church. Since he traveled a lot with his work, sometimes when the home teachers asked if they could come by, he would be gone. But the wife invited them to come and visit with her and the children anyway.

The first time that happened, the senior home teaching companion wondered if he should ask if they could pray with this woman as they finished their visit. He didn't wish to offend. But he decided he would at least ask. To his surprise, she readily agreed and asked him to offer the prayer. In the ensuing months, when he and his companion came to visit, the same scene repeated itself. She would never pray, nor would her children, but she always readily agreed and asked one of the home teachers to be voice.

On about the fourth or fifth such visit, when the home teacher asked, "Would it be all right if we offered a prayer before we leave?" her response totally caught him off guard. "Oh, yes," she said. "I love it when you pray. It leaves such a wonderful feeling in our home."

The fruits of the Spirit include happiness and peace.

"I Didn't Know God Made Them like That Anymore"

While we were doing a mission tour in the southern United States, a mission president and his wife were telling us about a recent baptism they had attended. The convert was an older man, a widower who lived alone and had been tracted out by the missionaries. The president said that this was the kind of man you would not have guessed would have responded well to missionaries. He tended to be a little crusty and gruff.

So, after the baptismal service, as the president and his wife were talking to this man—who, he said, was almost radiant with happiness—the president asked him this question, "So, Brother Jones, what was it that made you decide to listen to our missionaries?"

The man answered: "I live alone in a trailer house some distance outside of town. One day I was sitting in my living room watching television. From where I was sitting, I could see out my front window. Something caught my eye, and I turned to see two young men in white shirts and ties coming down the road that passed by my home. I was surprised because they were on foot and it was a hot day. To my further surprise, when they reached the gate of my little picket fence, they opened it and started up the walk. As I watched them come toward me, I looked them over carefully. As I did so, this thought came to me: 'I didn't know that God made young men like that anymore.' And so I let them in."

The fruits of the Spirit include hope and goodness.

SUMMARY

Here is the point about this particular function of the Holy Ghost. If you could ask those two missionaries, "Do you think you had the Spirit with you when you taught Brother Jones on that first day?" they would almost certainly say yes. But if you asked them *when* their teaching by the Spirit actually began, I'm pretty sure neither of them would have said, "As we came through the gate and started up the walk." Yet that was probably the most important teaching moment of that day because if it hadn't happened, nothing else would have followed.

If you asked the home teacher why that woman felt good, he

would likely say that she was feeling the Spirit. But if you said, "So would you say that you were 'teaching by the Spirit' while you were praying?" I think his reaction would likely be, "No, we had finished teaching her by that point." We don't normally think of the prayer as part of our "teaching time."

And if you were to ask those students who were interviewed to explain why they felt as they did about seminary, I don't think any of them would refer to the fruits of Spirit. Yet that was what they were feeling, so the Spirit was fulfilling His teaching function with those young people.

CHAPTER 10

STRIVING AND ENLIGHTENMENT

---+>•<+---

"DIRECTED AND GUIDED BY THE HOLY SPIRIT"

As Nephi reentered Jerusalem after several unsuccessful attempts to get the brass plates, putting his life in very real peril, he said: "And *I was led by the Spirit,* not knowing beforehand the things which I should do" (1 Nephi 4:6).

In the same scriptural passage in which the Lord gave us a list of the gifts of the Spirit, He also said this:

> It always has been given to the elders of my church from the beginning, and ever shall be, *to conduct all meetings as they are directed and guided by the Holy Spirit.* (D&C 46:2; see also Moroni 6:9)

I believe the phrase *all meetings* could include such nontraditional teaching settings as:

- A one-on-one conversation between parent and child
- A private counseling session between a priesthood leader and a member

- Missionaries stopping someone on the street to have a gospel conversation
- Young Women advisers sitting around a campfire chatting with their girls
- A telephone call of a mother to her son who is serving in the military in some far-off land
- A wide variety of other sessions in which faithful people interact with each other

Here are two wonderful ideals to strive for: to be led by the Spirit and to be directed and guided by the Spirit in all our "meetings." Either phrase would make a nice epitaph on one's gravestone:

- *She was led by the Spirit.*
- *Every meeting he ever conducted was directed and guided by the Spirit.*

These are two goals worthy of a lifetime of effort. I note them here as a reminder that we need to be careful that we don't, in our minds, try to limit the functions of the Holy Ghost—not *what* He does, not *where* He does it, not *when* He does it, and not *how* He does it.

With that in mind, here are some additional functions of the Holy Ghost that relate directly to teaching and preaching by the Spirit.

Function 5: The Holy Ghost Strives with Us

Ironically, this function of the Holy Ghost is most commonly expressed in the negative. In more than half a dozen places throughout the scriptures we find phrases like this: "My spirit shall not always strive with man" (Genesis 6:3; see also 1 Nephi 7:14; 2 Nephi 26:11; Mormon 5:16; Ether 2:15; D&C 1:33). This sobering warning usually describes those who have totally turned away from God and, as a result, have caused the Spirit to completely withdraw from their lives. But, even when expressed as a warning, this passage clearly points to a function of the Holy Ghost. If He sometimes ceases striving with individuals, that means that most of the time He *does* strive with us.

To *strive* means to work hard at something in order to accomplish one's purpose, to make diligent and vigorous effort to achieve a goal. Surely one of the functions of the Spirit is to strive continually to touch our hearts and turn us to God. This is always done in the

Many families struggle with wayward children. We can take comfort in "the eternal sealings of faithful parents" which will draw children "back to the fold" (Orson F. Whitney, in Conference Report, Apr. 1929, 110). We must never give up loving them, praying for them, and trusting in our Heavenly Father's care.

SUSAN W. TANNER,
"DID I TELL YOU . . . ?" 75

context of agency, of course. The Spirit never forces or coerces— but nevertheless, the Spirit makes every possible effort to influence us for good.

There surely is a lesson in that for parents, teachers, Church leaders, and disciples. The Father does not give up on His children at the first signs of rebellion. And so, even if those we love reject our efforts and turn away, we must follow the example of the Spirit and continue to strive with them. For that is what the Spirit will be doing.

Take the example of mothers. Even when their children turn away from them, do things that deeply hurt them, violate Church standards, and sometimes even end up behind bars, most mothers never stop praying for those children and reaching out to them.

They never, ever give up. This is true of many fathers, too, but mothers especially exhibit this remarkable trait.

This striving effort of the Spirit may not be quite as evident as when He gives us enlightenment, or helps us discern someone's thoughts and feelings, or comforts us, or brings us joy. But here are two examples of how the Spirit strives with an individual, and also what can happen if the individual refuses to heed those efforts.

What Had Compelled Me?

As I was thinking about how the Holy Ghost in His role as a teacher strives with individuals, I remembered an unusual experience my oldest daughter—now a mother of seven, including a missionary daughter—had on her mission in Hong Kong. I asked if she would share it. Here it is, in her words:

All my growing-up years I was very shy, quiet, and reserved. At school I liked to be invisible. I avoided situations with any kind of confrontation and would pay my younger sister a quarter to make phone calls for me. But despite all that, I had a great desire to serve a mission. I arrived in Hong Kong in August heat so dense I could hardly breathe. And after a day of orientation, I was put on a two-hour boat ride to a small Portuguese colony called Macau.

I was met at the boat dock by my Chinese companion, Sister Lui, whom I instantly loved for her warmth and cheerfulness. You can imagine how frightening it was for me to learn that because most people lived in high-rises with security systems, we did much of our contacting in parks, where we just walked up to people and started talking to them about the gospel. And of course this was to be done in Chinese, which only vaguely resembled the language I had learned in the MTC and in a class at BYU. I could not have been farther out of my comfort zone.

One day Sister Lui and I were in the park and she approached a group of *feijai*—teen and young adult gang members common in Hong Kong and Macau. They hang out in groups on the streets and in parks. Though their delinquent behaviors are not typically violent, I was still very nervous as we approached this bunch of ruffians.

They were in the middle of an arm-wrestling match, and it appeared the leader was asserting his authority by challenging and then winning the competition against each of the various members. My companion asked them if they would like to listen to a message. The leader pulled his cigarette out of his mouth, laughed, spat, and called us a derogatory name. My companion was angry, but as she turned to walk away I motioned to the leader that I wanted to challenge him to an arm wrestle. "I win—you listen," I stated in my limited Chinese.

My companion looked shocked. But I was more shocked than she was. What had compelled me to lay down this challenge? I had never been athletic or strong, let alone brave. Now in a foreign country I was going to arm wrestle these delinquent street guys? I couldn't understand the words in their response, but the meaning was clear. The gang leader would not stoop to arm wrestle this wimpy, foreign, religious woman, but for his amusement he assigned one of his gang members to pair up against me. I pinned the fellow's arm in a second, much to his humiliation amid the mocking from the group. The leader pointed to another, and then another. He picked progressively stronger members, and though each was more difficult than the last, I continued to win each successive match. Respect for me grew.

Finally the other gang members insisted that the leader must take me on. I could hear in his tone the words of bravado. He would show me. While he was crowing, I was praying in my heart with great fervency. As we put our arms up on the table, it was hushed. My companion looked nervous, probably rethinking the wisdom of letting her greenie missionary get involved in this. The wrestle was intense, leaning this way and that. I pushed and prayed and after a great struggle pinned the leader's arm to the table. "Now, you listen," I said with my sweetest smile.

I remember the sweet spirit that day in the park as my companion taught those young men about the gospel. I was touched to feel the Lord's love for them. My companion challenged them to come to church on Sunday. The following Sunday, we walked in just as the meeting was starting, accompanied by seven or eight of these gang members with their tattoos, tank tops, and cigarette reek.

Over time, most of the gang members dropped out of our discussions in the park, but one was eventually baptized. Who but Heavenly Father would know that an arm wrestle in the park would open the door to teaching His gospel? And who would have ever guessed that I would be the instrument in His hands?

To strive means to do something through consistent, prolonged, and vigorous effort; to labor for something without giving up. Think for a moment how many levels of striving by the Holy Ghost were exhibited in this case.

- The strong need our daughter felt to take a class in Chinese at BYU.
- Her desire to serve a mission, which at first she didn't want to do.
- Her assignment by a member of the Twelve to the Hong Kong mission.
- Having the gang of rowdies be in the park where the sister missionaries came to teach.
- The inspiration to throw out a challenge to arm wrestle the leader.
- The courage to act on an impression without hesitation.
- Choosing an approach that was probably the only way these arrogant and worldly young men would ever agree to listen to a message about Christ.
- The victories in the arm-wrestling contest.
- Her companion asking them to come to church that next Sunday, when it surely must have seemed a remote possibility that they would answer positively.
- The Spirit working on one of those young men until he was baptized and received the gift of the Holy Ghost for himself.

Truly, one of the functions of the Holy Ghost is to strive with individuals in hopes that they will open their hearts so that He can testify to them.

"Go to That House"

On the other hand, sometimes the Spirit withdraws because someone who has been given the gift of the Holy Ghost refuses to respond to His promptings. Here is another missionary example that is in sharp contrast with the previous one.

> While laboring in a city, my companion and I didn't receive a lot of referrals, so much of our time was spent

knocking on doors. We blocked the city into sections and then would systematically go through those sections until we had "tracted them out," as we called it. We started with the section that was closest to our apartment but had little success. After a week or two, we moved on to the next section, which was several blocks away. This meant that as we came and went from our apartment each day, we passed through that first section, sometimes as often as four times each day.

We had been doing this for several weeks when one day, as we were returning home for lunch, a nearby house that we passed by every day caught my attention. A feeling came quite clearly to me: "Go to that house. You need to knock on that door." I dismissed the thought, partly because we were hungry and anxious to get to our apartment, but partly because we had already "done this part of town." So I pushed the thought aside, and we passed on by.

> *The Spirit does not impose itself on an unwilling teacher or student. Resisted, it will quickly and simply withdraw.*
>
> Neal A. Maxwell,
> "Teaching by the Spirit," 3

But the feeling persisted. Each time we passed the home, the thought came back. "Go and knock on that door." Each time I ignored it, justifying myself by thinking it was just me being overzealous or that we were too busy. I actually would keep my eyes averted as we passed by to lessen the guilt. And I kept telling myself that these feelings were not really coming from the Spirit.

After two or three days of my pushing those feelings aside, they stopped coming. But the guilt didn't stop.

Finally, it got to be too much for me. I decided the only way to make the guilt go away was to do what I had been prompted to do. Coming home that next afternoon, I suddenly said to my companion: "We need to visit that house." He was surprised, but he didn't protest.

By this time, I guess I was half expecting one of those miraculous "missionary experiences" you hear about. The father or mother would throw open the door for us, take us inside, and insist that we teach them and their thirteen children, all of whom were over eight years old. We would set their baptismal date before we left and then immediately call the mission president and tell him about our "little miracle."

It didn't quite work out that way. Instead, there was no answer to our knock. The house was as silent as a tomb. For the next two weeks or so, we stopped again and again. Always the results were the same. It was like the house had been abandoned.

That's been many years ago now, yet I can still see that house in my mind. I can tell you what color the siding was and the color of the window trim. I still distinctly remember how those promptings felt, and I feel a stab of shame each time I think of how I brushed them aside. I have this nagging feeling that sometime in the world to come someone is going to come up to me and say, "Oh, yes. You're the missionary the Lord tried to get to come to our door, but you were too busy."

I used to think that when it said the Spirit doesn't always strive with men, it referred to when the people had become totally wicked, like with the Nephites or the Jaredites. Now I realize that we can do things that cause the Spirit to stop striving with us, both in individual instances and when we are teaching.

Function 6: The Holy Ghost Enlightens Us

Enlightenment is one of the most common ways the Spirit blesses our teaching and preaching efforts (see, for example, 1 Corinthians 2:9–11; D&C 6:14–15; 8:2–3; 11:13). Joseph Smith said, "The Holy Ghost is a revelator."[1] Revelation from God always involves the giving of light and knowledge. Thus enlightenment is a major function of the third member of the Godhead and also a major objective of teaching and preaching the gospel.[2] It comes as knowledge, wisdom, insights, understanding, and so on.

Here again, let us not limit our thinking only to formal classroom settings, though enlightenment does happen there often. Here are two quick examples of how this function is manifested, one in a classroom setting and one in the home.

"This Is Really Good Stuff"

A seminary teacher shared this experience he had one day in class:

> I was teaching a lesson that involved some pretty serious and deep gospel concepts. The class was going very well, with a lot of participation (both verbal and nonverbal) from the students. As I was wrapping up, one young woman raised her hand and asked me a question about what we had just learned. It was a profound question, one that I had never thought of before. I leaned back, thinking, "How do I answer that?" Then a thought came to me how I might diagram it. I picked up the chalk and stepped to the board. I said that what we had been talking about was more of a process than an event, and that perhaps we

could diagram that process as a flow chart. I began sketching boxes on the board, filling them with labels, then connecting them with arrows. As I neared my conclusion, I suddenly had this thought come very clearly: "Hey, this is really good stuff. This is a great answer." And I knew, at that moment, that it wasn't my answer. I knew that I had just experienced a moment where I had taught (and been taught) by the Spirit. It was a very humbling experience for me, an experience that I have never forgotten.

Barely in Time

Elder Dallin H. Oaks shared an experience of how enlightenment came when he was serving as president of Brigham Young University. It is also a good lesson on accepting the Lord's timing as well as His will.

> I had a choice experience with impelling revelation a few months after I began my service at BYU. As a new and inexperienced president, I had many problems to analyze and many decisions to reach. I was very dependent upon the Lord. One day in October 1971, I drove to a secluded area in Provo Canyon to ponder a particular problem. Although alone and without any interruption, I found myself unable to think of the problem at hand. Another pending issue *I was not yet ready to consider* kept thrusting itself into my mind: Should we modify BYU's academic calendar to complete the fall semester before Christmas?
>
> After ten or fifteen minutes of unsuccessful efforts to exclude thoughts of this subject, I finally realized what was happening. The issue of the calendar did not seem timely to me, and *I was certainly not seeking any guidance on it,* but the Spirit was trying to communicate with me on that

The Spirit of God speaking to the spirit of man has power to impart truth with greater effect and understanding than the truth can be imparted by personal contact even with heavenly beings. Through the Holy Ghost the truth is woven into the very fibre and sinews of the body so that it cannot be forgotten.

JOSEPH FIELDING SMITH,
DOCTRINES OF SALVATION, 1:47–48

subject. I immediately turned my full attention to that question and began to record my thoughts on a piece of paper. Within a few minutes I had recorded the details of a three-semester calendar, with all of its powerful advantages. Hurrying back to the campus, I reviewed these with my colleagues and found them enthusiastic. A few days later the board of trustees approved our proposed new calendar, and we published its dates, barely in time to make them effective in the fall of 1972.[3]

That is a wonderful example of how enlightening personal revelation comes. It is also an excellent illustration of two gifts of the Spirit mentioned earlier: the "differences of administration" and "the diversities of operations" (D&C 46:15–16).

Let us also remember that enlightenment often comes in the quiet moments of preparation, as well as during the actual time of performance.

CHAPTER 11

Power and Authority, Remembrance, and Knowing What to Say in the Very Hour

Up to this point we have examined six functions of the Spirit, some in great detail. Hopefully, you are beginning to sense how critical these and other functions are to our understanding of what it means to preach and teach by the Spirit. Here are three additional functions and roles of the Holy Ghost.

Function 7: The Holy Ghost Gives Power and Authority to What We Teach and When We Testify

In the Bible Dictionary we have this statement about faith: "Faith is kindled by hearing the testimony of those who have faith."[1] Paul taught the Romans: "Faith cometh by hearing, and hearing by the word of God" (Romans 10:17). The Prophet Joseph, keying off of Paul's statement, made this clear declaration: "Faith comes by hearing the word of God, through the testimony of the servants of God; *that testimony is always attended by the Spirit of prophecy and revelation.*"[2]

We have already noted that a major function of the Spirit is to testify. But He also inspires us to testify so that He can whisper, "Listen to what they're saying. What you are hearing is true."

In other words, when we testify in faith, then the Holy Ghost can give a second and more important witness, validating what the listeners have heard.

Even if the hearer rejects what is presented, the Spirit still gives a special power and validity to the testimony of one who faithfully preaches and teaches. For this reason, parents and teachers and leaders are encouraged to bear testimony each time they teach the gospel. This gives opportunity for the Spirit to bear witness to the listener that what he or she is hearing is true. The scriptures provide several remarkable examples of this.

You [may] remember an occasion when two tuning forks were selected which were calibrated to the same wavelength, and one of them was set up in one part of the room and the other thirty or forty feet away. Someone struck the first tuning fork, and people put their ear to the second, and it vibrated and made the same sound as the first one. This is an illustration . . . [of] what is involved in speaking by the Spirit. Somebody who is in tune with the Spirit speaks words that are heard by the power of the Spirit.

Bruce R. McConkie,
"The Foolishness of Teaching," 9

The Prophets Testify of the Power and Authority of Their Office

Note how often the preaching and teaching of various prophets are described in the scriptures in terms of both "power and authority":

- *Micah.* "Truly I am full of power by the spirit of the Lord, and of judgment, and of might, to declare unto Jacob his transgression, and to Israel his sin" (Micah 3:8).
- *Joshua.* "Have not I commanded thee? Be strong and of a

good courage; be not afraid, neither be thou dismayed: for the Lord thy God is with thee whithersoever thou goest" (Joshua 1:9).

- *Lehi.* "And it came to pass that my father did speak unto [Laman and Lemuel] in the valley of Lemuel, with power, being filled with the Spirit, until their frames did shake before him. And he did confound them, that they durst not utter against him; wherefore, they did as he commanded them" (1 Nephi 2:14).

- *Nephi.* "If [my words] are not the words of Christ, judge ye—for Christ will show unto you, with power and great glory, that they are his words, at the last day; and you and I shall stand face to face before his bar; and ye shall know that I have been commanded of him to write these things, notwithstanding my weakness" (2 Nephi 33:11).

- *King Benjamin.* "Behold, king Benjamin was a holy man, and he did reign over his people in righteousness; and there were many holy men in the land, and they did speak the word of God with power and with authority" (Words of Mormon 1:17).

- *Moroni.* "And I exhort you to remember these things; for the time speedily cometh that ye shall know that I lie not, for ye shall see me at the bar of God; and the Lord God will say unto you: Did I not declare my words unto you, which were written by this man, like as one crying from the dead, yea, even as one speaking out of the dust?" (Moroni 10:27).

This gift is not just for prophets who lead the Church. We are told of some young missionaries who paid the required spiritual price and achieved that same kind of authority and power in their missionary service. Alma said of the sons of Mosiah:

They had waxed strong in the knowledge of the truth; for they were men of a sound understanding and they had searched the scriptures diligently, that they might know the word of God. But this is not all; they had given themselves to much prayer, and fasting; therefore they had the spirit of prophecy, and the spirit of revelation, *and when they taught, they taught with power and authority of God.* (Alma 17:2–3)

Here is another powerful model for us to emulate. Just prior to Christ's coming, the prophet in the land of Zarahemla was Nephi, the grandson of Helaman. A short time before the great destruction in the Americas, we are told that Nephi "began to testify, boldly" (3 Nephi 7:16). The result is truly remarkable. "And it came to pass that they were angry with him, even because he had greater *power* than they, for *it were not possible that they could disbelieve his words*" (3 Nephi 7:18).

O, that every teacher in the Church, every missionary called to serve, every priesthood and auxiliary leader, every parent and grandparent could have it said of them: "They taught with the power and authority of God, to the point where it was not possible that others could disbelieve their words."

Function 8: The Holy Ghost Brings Things to Our Remembrance

On the night before His death, as the Savior was teaching the Twelve for the last time in His mortal ministry, He spoke of the Holy Ghost and made them two promises:

The Comforter, which is the Holy Ghost, whom the Father will send in my name, he shall teach you all things, and bring all things to your remembrance, whatsoever I have said unto you. (John 14:26)

We have already spoken about how the Holy Ghost in His role as teacher gives us knowledge, understanding, wisdom, and enlightenment. That function is reiterated here. But in addition, Jesus promised that the Holy Ghost would also help His disciples remember His words. This promise is also extended to us who are striving to serve in the kingdom, to teach the gospel, to counsel others, and to bless His children.

It has been my experience that teachers in all settings frequently experience this particular gift of the Spirit. Perhaps the remembrance will involve a previously overlooked scriptural reference. Perhaps a story or an example that is especially relevant will come into our minds. Quotes from the Brethren may suddenly pop into our heads at just the right moment.

> *A wise man has said that we need to be reminded more than we need to be instructed. One of the most powerful functions of the Spirit is to bring things to our remembrance.*
>
> NEAL A. MAXWELL, "TEACHING BY THE SPIRIT," 2

Following are some examples of how the Spirit brings things to our remembrance so we can teach with greater power and authority.

Memories of the Spirit

As I began writing this section, two things were brought to my remembrance. I remembered a quote by President Joseph F. Smith that I hadn't thought about for a long time. Here is what he said about remembering:

All those salient truths which come home so forcibly to the head and heart seem but *the awakening of the memories*

93

of the spirit. Can we know anything here that we did not know before we came?[3]

And with that quote came another example. This time I remembered a story shared with my wife and me by one of our mission presidents while we were serving in Europe. He told of a wonderful family that was brought into the Church by the missionaries. After their baptism, the father wrote a letter to the president and his wife. In it he made this interesting observation:

"On the day our family made the commitment to be baptized, I said, with some wonder, to the missionaries, 'I've never been a religious man. I didn't go to church as a child. I guess I believed in God, but I never thought much about Him and never prayed. But when you were teaching us the discussions, I had the strangest feeling that I already knew what you were teaching us. Over and over it all sounded so familiar to me.'"

Here are some additional examples.

I Promised My Teacher

Sometimes the remembrance may come long after the event occurs. This story was shared with me by a bishop who had it told to him by one of his ward members.

When I was in high school, I was big into football and thought I was really hot stuff. I was using bad language and had even started to break the Word of Wisdom with all my football buddies. My parents didn't know any of this, of course, and insisted that I attend seminary. I skipped class often, but I didn't dare do it too much for fear my parents would find out about it and make me quit football.

One day in class, we were talking about serving

94

full-time missions. By that time, I had already made my decision. A mission wasn't going to be part of my life.

Then my seminary teacher did something completely unexpected. "I would like to see by show of hands," he said to the class, "how many of you young men will promise me that you will serve a full-time mission when the time comes." I looked up, completely caught off guard. Every boy's hand was up except mine, and several were looking at me. I wasn't about to be the odd man out, so I raised my hand, even though I knew full well it was a lie. There was no way I was going to be a missionary.

Two years later I found myself with the United States Army on the island of Guam in the Pacific. I hadn't been to church since I left home. I was smoking and drinking. One evening I was sitting out on the beach all by myself, smoking a cigarette and thinking about home. Out of the blue came this thought: "You promised your seminary teacher that you would go on a mission." I almost laughed out loud. "Me? On a mission?" But I couldn't get it out of my head. It came back to me over and over. I had promised my teacher.

Some of the time your efforts will be met with indifference. I know also, however, that for many of your students you are in fact planting little intellectual and spiritual time bombs, and the implantation is so subtle that you'll wonder if in fact you have connected at all. And then someday, when the circumstances are right, there will be in them an explosion or reminding relevancy from that implantation from your instruction.

Neal A. Maxwell, "The Old Testament: Relevancy within Antiquity," 7

By the time I completed my tour of duty with the army a year later, I had stopped smoking and drinking and

95

was going to church. When I returned home, I went to the bishop and told him I wanted to put my life in order and serve a mission. He was almost as surprised as I was. But I went, thanks to a teacher who asked us to raise our hands and make a commitment in seminary.

Wouldn't it be wonderful if somehow that seminary teacher came to know that his simple request for a commitment came to fruition after several years? How gratifying that would be, to know that something you did had had such a powerful impact on the mind of a wandering soul! It is more likely that he will never know, but that doesn't lessen the little miracle that he initiated that day. As he taught by the Spirit, the Spirit implanted it into that boy's mind to be recalled much, much later.

Teaching about Tithing

Here is another wonderful story from a sister missionary:

We had been teaching Shellie and felt she was golden. She was a member of another Christian faith, but she had been receptive to the fulness of the gospel. Then we taught her about tithing. When we explained that the Lord commanded us to pay 10 percent of our income, she was upset. "That is too much! My church just asks us to give what we can. There is no quota on what we pay! Your church is greedy and unrealistic."

I could tell tithing was going to be a deal breaker for her. I prayed in my heart, "What can I say?" Then I remembered the story about Abraham paying tithing to Melchizedek and I was prompted to read that story to her. The story was hazy in my mind at best, and I knew it wasn't marked in my scriptures. I quickly turned to the Topical Guide under tithing. "Let's turn to Genesis

14:18–20," I said after a moment. After we read about Abraham paying tithes, I testified about something I didn't even know myself until that moment: "You see, Shellie," I said, "tithing is a principle that was established anciently by the Lord and remains in effect even until today."

The Spirit then came and testified to her that this principle was true. She asked, "But if Abraham paid tithing, and God has always commanded his people to pay tithing, then why doesn't my church require that?"

Shellie was baptized a short time later. The last I heard she was serving as Young Women president in her ward.

Function 9: The Holy Ghost Gives Us What to Say in the Very Hour and Moment of Our Need

There are several places in the scriptures where this promise is mentioned.

- Nephi taught that if we "feast upon the words of Christ," they "will tell you all things what ye should do" (2 Nephi 32:3).
- In a revelation given to missionaries, the Lord was very specific about this promise: "Neither take ye thought beforehand[4] what ye shall say; but treasure up in your minds continually the words of life, and *it shall be given you in the very hour* that portion that shall be meted unto every man" (D&C 84:85).
- The promise is repeated again in another revelation: "Lift up your voices unto this people; speak the thoughts that I shall put into your hearts, and you shall not be confounded before men; For it shall be given you in the very hour, *yea, in the very moment,* what ye shall say" (D&C 100:5–6; see also Matthew 10:19; D&C 31:11).

"It's Not My Meeting"

It was Sunday morning and time to leave for sacrament meeting. As the father and mother were rounding up the children and sending them to the car, their fourteen-year-old son didn't appear. The father went to the head of the stairs and called down at him to hurry up or they were going to be late. After a moment, the boy stepped into view in jeans and a T-shirt, saying, "I don't want to go to sacrament meeting today." The father told him that was not the issue and to hurry up and change his clothes.

"I'm not going," the son said defiantly, "and you can't make me."

"Oh, yeah?" snapped the father angrily, and started down the stairs. Then suddenly came this thought: *If this were the Savior, how would He deal with this boy?* And almost instantly came the answer. He stopped and looked at his son. "Why are you telling *me* this?" he said. "It's not *my* meeting. It's Heavenly Father's meeting. So you go down and tell your other Father that you don't want to go to His meeting."

With that, the father turned and went back up the stairs to get the rest of the family into the car. A few moments later, he heard his son call out, "All right, all right! Give me a minute. I'm coming."

"Some days later," the father concluded, "when I read the promise about the Lord giving us what to say in the very hour of our need, I added these words to the scriptural promise: "Yea, even unto rebellious teenagers."

Earlier, we used the story of the teacher who received revelation as he tried to answer a difficult question for a student. We included that as an example of the gift of enlightenment. That story could just have easily been used as an example of receiving inspiration at the very moment we need it.

Earlier, we told the story of the missionaries who were being verbally hammered by the woman who thought they were the devil's emissaries. We used that story to illustrate the gift of testimony. That example could just have easily been used here as an example of the gift of being given what to say in a time of need.

The point is, this particular gift occurs more frequently than we may at first suppose. Once we have clearly defined it, we may find numerous examples of when it has been manifested in our own teaching and learning experiences.

CHAPTER 12

An Increase in Skills
and Abilities

——+>••<+——

There is one more function of the Holy Ghost we need to discuss. Don't be surprised if this function comes as a bit of a surprise. It did for me when I first came across it. This was something I had not considered as part of teaching or preaching by the Spirit.

Function 10: The Spirit Can Help Increase One's Skills and Abilities

When I first started searching the scriptures for information on the functions of the Holy Ghost, one scripture in the Old Testament really took me aback. It was part of a lengthy set of instructions given to Moses on how to build a tabernacle—a portable temple—for Israel.

The Lord was very specific about how this was to be done. Moses was told how the building was to be laid out and constructed. But that was not all. He was told what materials were to be used throughout. Instructions were given on the furnishings and where they were to be placed. Even colors were specified in some cases. In addition, detailed and specific instructions were given for the clothing that was to be worn by the officiating priests.

These instructions take nearly twelve pages in the book of Exodus (see chapters 25–30). Considering that Israel was wandering in a desert wilderness at the time, this must have seemed like a daunting task to Moses and his people, who had been slaves in Egypt. How were they ever to accomplish such a thing?

It was in that detailed set of instructions that I found a reference to the Spirit that startled me.

Some of the great bishops of my lifetime include a brickmason, a grocer, a farmer, a dairyman, and one who ran an ice cream business. What any may have lacked in formal education was insignificant. They were humble men, and because they were humble they were taught and magnified by the Holy Spirit. Without exception they were greatly strengthened as they learned to labor diligently to fulfill their callings and to minister to the Saints. . . . So it is with all of the callings in the Church.

James E. Faust,
Finding Light in a Dark World, 121

And the Lord spake unto Moses, saying, See, I have called by name Bezaleel the son of Uri, the son of Hur, of the tribe of Judah: *And I have filled him with the spirit of God,* in wisdom, and in understanding, and in knowledge, and *in all manner of workmanship,* To *devise* cunning works, to *work* in gold, and in silver, and in brass, And in *cutting* of stones, to *set* them, and in *carving* of timber, *to work in all manner of workmanship.* (Exodus 31:1–5)

It is not surprising that Bezaleel, who was to be the head craftsman on the project, was promised increased wisdom, understanding, and knowledge. But he was also promised increased skills and abilities. And these were skills in complicated and highly

101

challenging areas of workmanship. A few chapters later, after the work had begun, we find this note:

> Then *wrought* Bezaleel and Aholiab, and every wise hearted man, in whom the Lord put wisdom and understanding *to know how to work all manner of work* for the service of the sanctuary. (Exodus 36:1)

I still remember how I marveled at this unexpected function of the Spirit. Then came this question: "Okay, so this is a function of the Spirit, but does it have anything to do with teaching?" That was an easy answer. Of course it did. Think again of our definition of teaching and preaching by the Spirit.

> *Teaching by the Spirit takes place when the Holy Ghost is fulfilling His role and His functions with either the teacher or the learner or both.*

As recorded in Exodus, the Spirit was definitely teaching Bezaleel and Aholiab how to be better craftsmen. But Bezaleel and Aholiab couldn't do it all. Apprentices and workmen were called, and they too had to be taught the skills and to receive similar gifts from the Spirit.

And with that, I began looking for other examples of when the Spirit enhanced individual skills and abilities. Here are just a few.

Exceedingly Fine

Though Nephi was given a completely different kind of project, he was perhaps even more unprepared and unqualified than Bezaleel and Aholiab. When Lehi's colony finally reached the seashore and faced the challenge of crossing the ocean to the promised land, Nephi was told by the Lord to build a ship. What a staggering thing that must have been to a young man who had zero experience in shipbuilding. And not only would he need to know *how* to build a ship—an enormous task in and of itself—but he would also need high-level skills in such areas as naval architecture, engineering, carpentry, woodworking, sail making, and dozens of other fields of expertise. Remember, this had to be a ship seaworthy enough to go halfway around the world.

But Nephi had already learned to say, "I will go and do the things which the Lord hath commanded" (1 Nephi 3:7). So, trusting in the Lord, he went to work. He didn't travel to the nearest port city and ask to apprentice on with a shipbuilding company. He didn't send to one of those centers and ask for skilled help. He chose a different preparation strategy:

> Now I, Nephi, did not work the timbers after the manner which was learned by men, neither did I build the ship after the manner of men; but I did build it after the manner which the Lord had shown unto me; wherefore, *it was not after the manner of men.* And I, Nephi, did go into the mount oft, and I did pray oft unto the Lord; wherefore *the Lord showed unto me great things.* (1 Nephi 18:2–3)

No wonder Laman and Lemuel thought he was mad. But when the ship was finished, even those two hardheaded skeptics had to admit that "the workmanship was exceedingly fine" (1 Nephi 18:4). Noah and the brother of Jared are two other examples of this remarkable kind of building achievement.[1]

Teaching Skills

In the list of the gifts of the Spirit, the Lord specifically includes the gift of teaching (see D&C 46:18). This would suggest that the Spirit can help us improve our teaching ability and skills. We need to be careful here, for we are not suggesting that only skilled teachers are able to teach by the Spirit. The Spirit can fulfill

His functions even if the teacher may be a little dull or not as effective as others in explaining things.

Elder Dallin H. Oaks put it this way:

> If we have the Spirit of the Lord to guide us, we can teach any person, no matter how well educated, any place in the world. The Lord knows more than any of us, and if we are his servants, acting under his Spirit, he can deliver his message of salvation to each and every soul.[2]

But I think we also recognize that there are what we often call "gifted teachers" in the Church. Isn't it possible that in addition to the help they receive in *what* to teach, they may also be blessed by the Spirit in *how* they teach it? For example, the Spirit may play a role in how they express themselves, the methods they use to catch and hold the interest of their listeners, their ability to simplify complex concepts, or their capacity to find excellent examples to illustrate their points.

And by that same token, since the Lord invites us to "seek ye earnestly the best gifts" (D&C 46:8), surely it would not be improper for a gospel teacher to seek that gift of teaching for himself or herself. Here are some examples of the Lord's increasing an individual's ability to preach and teach.

Of course there are individuals who are keeping their covenants who lack teaching charisma. Of course there are those whose lives are in order who are not exciting as teachers. However, the Spirit blesses the efforts of all who live worthily. It endorses what they say or do. There is a witnessing authenticity which proceeds from the commandment keeper, which speaks for itself. Therefore, I prefer doctrinal accuracy and spiritual certitude (even with a little dullness) to charisma with unanchored cleverness.

NEAL A. MAXWELL,
"TEACHING BY THE SPIRIT," 5

I Am Slow of Speech

Early in the history of the world, the Lord called Enoch to be His prophet. Enoch's reaction was not unlike that of many of us when a calling of great responsibility comes.

> And when Enoch had heard these words, he bowed himself to the earth, before the Lord, and spake before the Lord, saying: Why is it that I have found favor in thy sight, and am but a lad, and all the people hate me; for I am slow of speech; wherefore am I thy servant?" (Moses 6:31)

This lack of self-confidence and those feelings of inadequacy may have been normal, but they were not acceptable to the Lord.

> And the Lord said unto Enoch: Go forth and do as I have commanded thee, and no man shall pierce thee. Open thy mouth, and it shall be filled, and *I will give thee utterance.*" (Moses 6:32)

Just how fully was that promise fulfilled? Note two later passages that describe Enoch's teaching abilities:

> And as Enoch *spake forth the words of God,* the people trembled, and could not stand in his presence. (Moses 6:47).

> And so great was the faith of Enoch that he led the people of God, and their enemies came to battle against them; and *he spake the word of the Lord,* and the earth trembled, and the mountains fled; . . . *so powerful*

If any . . . feel unprepared— even incapable—of responding to a call to serve, to sacrifice, to bless the lives of others, remember this truth: "Whom God calls, God qualifies." He who notes the sparrow's fall will not abandon the servant's need.

THOMAS S. MONSON,
LIVE THE GOOD LIFE, 17

was the word of Enoch, and so great was the power of the language which God had given him. (Moses 7:13)

"Who Hath Made Man's Mouth?"

In what must have been a painful thing for him to recount later, Moses wrote of his own reaction to his call. He actually protested to the Lord not once, but several times. To help calm his fears, the Lord gave Moses two miraculous signs that he could use to convince Israel that his call was from God (see Exodus 4:1–10). But even that wasn't enough for Moses. "And Moses said unto the Lord, O my Lord, I am not eloquent, . . . but I am slow of speech, and of a slow tongue."

That brought a sharp rebuke. "And the Lord said unto him, Who hath made man's mouth? or who maketh the dumb, or deaf, or the seeing, or the blind? have not I the Lord? Now therefore go, and *I will be with thy mouth,* and teach thee what thou shalt say" (Exodus 4:10–12). Finally, Moses went and did as commanded, and the rest is history. (See Jeremiah 1:5–9 for another example of this.)

To summarize, although it may be natural to have feelings of being unprepared, unworthy, or unable to fulfill a call from the Lord, those are not acceptable excuses. Such expressions can actually offend the Spirit.

Note this stern warning the Lord gave to the early Saints: "Who am I that made man, saith the Lord, that will hold him guiltless that obeys not my commandments? Who am I, saith the Lord, that have promised and have not fulfilled?" (D&C 58:30–31). One week later, the Lord added this:

> With some I am not well pleased, for they will not
> open their mouths, but they hide the talent which I have
> given unto them, because of the fear of man. Wo unto

such, for mine anger is kindled against them. And it shall come to pass, if they are not more faithful unto me, it shall be taken away, even that which they have. (D&C 60:2–3)

Summary

Failings and weaknesses are part of our mortal experience. So are feelings of inadequacy, lack of ability, and the sense of forever falling short. This is true not just of our service in the kingdom but in our personal and professional lives as well. How grateful we should be that the Lord accepts our imperfections and gives us the Spirit as our companion. Not only does the Holy Ghost give us knowledge and inspiration to guide and help and protect us, but He can also increase our skills, magnify our abilities, expand our efforts, and enhance our performance.

We have looked at examples of faithful men who doubted their abilities and questioned the Lord's judgment, yet went on to play critical roles in God's work. We also saw an example of one who, even in the face of an incredibly difficult physical task, simply trusted in the Lord and went forward. Nephi is an example to us all.

Another equally remarkable example of the proper response to a call, even if it is completely overwhelming, comes not from one of the prophets but from a humble young woman from the little town of Nazareth. Her response to a calling of such stunning magnitude that it must surely have seemed impossible is a marvelous example of faith, trust, and humble submission. After being told by the angel Gabriel that she was to be the mother of the Messiah, who was also going to be the Son of God, her first question—a very natural one—was how this was possible, since she was not married. But once Gabriel explained that to her, her response serves as a perfect model for all of us: *"Behold the handmaid of the Lord; be it unto me according to thy word"* (Luke 1:38).

I shall close this chapter with a sweet experience my wife and I had while serving in the Area Presidency in Europe. We were holding a stake conference in Wales. In the Sunday session, a new stake Relief Society president was sustained. The stake president had asked if it would be all right to have the outgoing Relief Society president speak as part of conference. He told me what a remarkable woman she was and of the service she had rendered. He wanted the members of the stake to hear from her; I agreed. She gave a wonderful talk—very uplifting, very faith-inspiring.

When the conference was over, my wife and I went over to her and thanked her for her talk and for her service. She told us how grateful she was for her experience and how much she had learned from it. Then she said something that made us laugh and at the same time struck a poignant chord in both Lynn and me.

"I was sustained in stake conference three years ago," she said. "Elder Neal A. Maxwell was the presiding authority that day." She started to tear up. "Afterward, Elder Maxwell came up to me to congratulate me on my new calling. By that time, I was feeling totally overwhelmed. 'Oh, Elder Maxwell,' I cried, 'I feel so inadequate, so unqualified.'

"He smiled at me, then softly said, 'Oh? You too?'"

PART III

The Principles in Action

CHAPTER 13

ANSWERING THE QUESTIONS

———◆•◆———

Here is a summary of things we have learned up to this point:

- As a Church we are charged to preach and teach the gospel to the world. This constitutes a major part of the work we do in the kingdom.
- We are to preach and teach the gospel by the Spirit so that all are edified. If we don't have the Spirit, this will not happen.
- We proposed a working definition of teaching by the Spirit that ties it directly to the roles and functions of the Holy Ghost.
- We defined and explored ten functions of the Holy Ghost that are directly related to teaching.

With these principles, we can now answer the questions and clarify the misunderstandings discussed in chapter 4.

What is it that a teacher does when he or she is teaching by the

Spirit? Will a teacher always know if he or she has taught by the Spirit? Will the learner?

Using our definition of teaching by the Spirit, the answer to that question is clear. A teacher—which includes classroom teachers, parents, leaders, home and visiting teachers, and individuals— does those things that invite the Spirit into the teaching setting and allow the Spirit to fulfill its functions as teacher with both the teacher and learner. This can involve just about any kind of action or behavior that is in harmony with gospel principles. One teaches, inspires, discerns, corrects, rebukes, testifies—or, on occasion, remains silent— edifies, prepares carefully, speaks spontaneously, laughs, weeps, and shows forth love, patience, longsuffering, and so on.

> *Because we need the Holy Ghost, we must be cautious and careful not to go beyond teaching true doctrine. The Holy Ghost is the Spirit of Truth. His confirmation is invited by our avoiding speculation or personal interpretation. . . . One of the surest ways to avoid even getting near false doctrine is to choose to be simple in our teaching.*
>
> HENRY B. EYRING,
> *BECAUSE HE FIRST LOVED US,* 118

There is not a set formula, nor are there only one or two patterns of behavior. Sometimes the Spirit functions with both the teacher and the learner at the same time. Other times it is one or the other. And often the Spirit is teaching us individually outside of a formal teaching setting. This is what we mean by "learning by the Spirit."

But will the teacher or the learner always know when that is happening? No. In fact, it is not uncommon for the Spirit to be fulfilling its functions with the teacher and/or the learner without either of them being consciously aware of it. Think of the example of the young soldier remembering that he promised his seminary teacher he would serve a mission. Even when those feelings came, he didn't identify them as coming from the Spirit, only that he couldn't get them out of his mind. The following story, shared with me by a colleague at BYU, provides another example.

Create Your Own Spiritual Destiny

I was teaching a class on the Pearl of Great Price at BYU. We had just started our study of the book of Abraham. We were reading the first few verses together and commenting on how Abraham had nearly been sacrificed to the Egyptian gods. His father was cooperating with the priests in a ritual that would end with the death of his son. But we didn't say more than that about the father. Our focus was on how an angel had intervened and saved Abraham's life.

I felt like the class went very well. We had a good discussion with lots of participation. I was pleased. Then, as class ended, a young man stopped to talk with me. "Brother Jones," he said, "that was a great lesson today. Thank you very much for what you taught us. It was very significant for me personally." Curious, I asked him what particular point had impressed him. "That we can create our own spiritual destiny," he responded. I wasn't sure exactly what he meant by that, so I asked him to explain. The young man said that he was a recent convert who came from a highly dysfunctional family. His father especially had been a very negative influence in his life. "As we were reading together," he went on, "I realized that Abraham father's was a pretty destructive parent too. Then came this thought: 'It doesn't matter that your family was dysfunctional. You, like Abraham, can create your own spiritual destiny.'"

That's a sweet example of being taught by the Spirit, but here is the point. My friend, chuckling softly, concluded, "I had not mentioned that concept in any way. It was a powerful teaching moment for this young man, but it didn't come from me."

What will the learner be experiencing or feeling if a teacher is teaching by the Spirit?

Learners will be experiencing one or more of the various functions of the Spirit, such as enlightenment, understanding, comfort, hope, peace, or joy. But that doesn't automatically mean that they will be consciously aware of what is happening. Even though teaching by the Spirit is occurring, it doesn't mean it will always be noticed or recognized for what it is. Also, remember the analogy of edification as a building process. In many cases, the "house" may not be aware at all that another "brick" has just been put in place.

Is it possible that the Holy Ghost may not be present in a teaching setting but the teacher or learner thinks that He is?

This may not be common, but it does happen. There is false revelation.[1] Elder Packer warned:

> Be ever on guard lest you be deceived by inspiration from an unworthy source. You can be given false spiritual messages. There are counterfeit spirits just as there are counterfeit angels. . . . The spiritual part of us and the emotional part of us are so closely linked that *it is possible to mistake an emotional impulse for something spiritual.*[2]

Here are just a few examples of how mistaking false revelation for true might happen. We may be moved to tears by an emotional story or example and think that is the Spirit touching our hearts, when in reality it may just be a sad or touching story. Some students may love their class or their teacher because it is "so much fun," but they are learning very little of substance there. A teacher may say something so intellectually stimulating that it really "wows" those who hear it, and they assume that it must therefore be true. In reality, it could be patently false. Some highly skilled speakers can stimulate (some might even say manipulate) various emotions by what they say and how they say it. Those emotions may or may not be coming from the Spirit.

To push the point a little, here are some scriptural examples of some highly "effective" teachers, if "effectiveness" is defined strictly by teaching and communicating skills and ability:

I think if we are not careful . . . , we may begin to try to counterfeit the true influence of the Spirit of the Lord by unworthy and manipulative means. I get concerned when it appears that strong emotion or free-flowing tears are equated with the presence of the Spirit. Certainly the Spirit of the Lord can bring strong emotional feelings, including tears, but that outward manifestation ought not to be confused with the presence of the Spirit itself.

HAROLD B. LEE,
"ETERNAL INVESTMENTS," 3

- Sherem was said to have "a perfect knowledge of the language of the people" and "much power of speech, according to the power of the devil" (Jacob 7:4).
- Nehor, who taught the people many false doctrines, was so effective that "many did believe on his words, even so many that they began to support him and give him money" (Alma 1:5).
- Zeezrom was "expert in the devices of the devil" (Alma 11:21).
- Korihor, the anti-Christ, taught so persuasively that he even led former members of the Church to "lift up their heads [that is, to be proud] in their wickedness" (Alma 30:18).
- The history of the Church is filled with examples of crazed

mobs that were whipped into an emotional frenzy by ministers of local churches.

- Jesus taught the Twelve that the time would come when men would seek to kill them and would think that *they were doing God a service* (see John 16:2).

I remember talking with a recent convert who said that his former church held anti-Mormon seminars for its members. He had attended several. One of the things they were taught was that the Book of Mormon was a product of the devil. Therefore, the very book itself was infused with an evil power. Even touching the book could pull an individual into Satan's power. If missionaries offered them a Book of Mormon, they were not even to touch it lest they be overcome by the powers of darkness.

> *Beware of false prophets, who come to you in sheep's clothing, but inwardly they are ravening wolves.*
>
> 3 NEPHI 14:15;
> SEE ALSO MATTHEW 7:15

Those are other examples, which illustrate that we cannot assume that because something is being done under the pretense of being good, or because "it feels good," or "feels right," it is automatically coming from the Spirit.

Can a teacher really create a true spiritual experience for the learner?

When teachers think that it is their responsibility to create spiritual experiences for others, their intentions may be good, but that doesn't change the fact that this is not a correct concept. As teachers, leaders, and parents, we want to do something that touches the hearts of others and strengthens their faith and testimony. Spiritual experiences are one of the best ways to do that. But providing spiritual experiences for others is not *our* function. It is not possible for one person to give another person a true spiritual experience. Only the Spirit can do that, and He does it under the direction of the Father and the Son.

A teacher, parent, or Church leader can say or do things to help create a climate where learners are more likely to have spiritual experiences, but we must be careful that we do not inadvertently take credit for what only the Spirit can do. These are not our gifts, and we must take care that we don't offend the Spirit by taking credit for His functions. Moses, for all of his righteousness and a lifetime of faithful service, was sharply rebuked when he momentarily forgot himself and, with a slip of the tongue, took personal credit for providing water for his people by striking a rock (see Numbers 20:7–13).

> *Praying, holding family home evenings, and studying the scriptures with our children are important foundations. As we strive to create a spiritual environment, our family members can be led to those experiences that will help them build their own personal testimonies.*
>
> JOE J. CHRISTENSEN,
> ONE STEP AT A TIME, 92

What constitutes a true spiritual experience for an individual?

A true spiritual experience is most easily defined as any experience—whether we recognize it as such or not—where the Holy Spirit interacts with us in such a way that He is fulfilling His various functions and purposes with either the teacher or the learner. Normally, this involves some kind of response from the individual indicating that he or she is touched or moved by the Spirit. This can happen across a broad range of experiences that vary greatly in intensity, directness, and visibility. Some are so subtle we may not recognize them at all. Therefore, it is possible for a person—either teacher or learner—to have a true spiritual experience and not identify it for what it is. In some cases the person may not know it until sometime after it occurred.

Another defining aspect of any experience that comes from the Spirit is that it will edify. It will uplift, enlighten, strengthen, warn, comfort, instruct, bless, and bring spiritual growth. As Mormon taught his son Moroni, the way to tell whether something comes from God through the Spirit is simple: "That which is of God inviteth and enticeth to do good continually; wherefore, every thing which inviteth and enticeth to do good, and to love God, and to serve him, is inspired of God" (Moroni 7:13).

Can a teacher be teaching by the Spirit and yet it has no effect, or even a negative effect, on the student?

We have already answered that question in part, but here again we can answer with a clear and definite yes. The learner always has individual agency. Thus an individual may reject spiritual promptings and feelings for a whole variety of reasons—disinterest, preoccupation with other things, rebellion, immaturity, being caught up in the cares of the world, and so on. Because of that, people can also choose how to respond. They can believe or mock, accept or reject, be touched with love and gratitude or grow angry and disgusted. (For further discussion on this, see the next chapter.)

Can the learner be taught by the Spirit even if the teacher doesn't have the Spirit?

Again, of course. Remember that none of us can dictate or set limits on what the Spirit may or may not do. Agency is always a major factor operating in the teacher, too. Teachers may fail to prepare, or be unworthy in their personal lives, or do things in the teaching setting that grieve the Spirit. Some may even be those wolves masquerading in sheep's clothing of which the Savior spoke. But that doesn't mean that learners will automatically be at the mercy of a teacher's folly. Here is an example of just such a situation.

Find Out for Yourself

A recently returned missionary was taking a college ethics course from a caustic, skeptical professor who openly bragged that he found the idea of God and organized religion quite ridiculous. To support his position, often he would read selected Bible passages to the students and then proceed to show how ludicrous or self-contradictory they were. The young woman admitted that some of the arguments were pretty persuasive and caused her to begin to wonder if there were any truth in what the professor was saying.

One day, as the professor was really laying it on heavily, there came this thought into the student's mind: "What he is saying is not true. He is taking those passages out of context, or twisting the meaning of the original writer to mean something quite different than was intended. You need to study those passages yourself and see if he is correct." She followed that prompting and later bore witness that not only did she find the professor to be deliberately misleading, but the passages actually strengthened her faith and testimony about God.

What can a teacher do to create a climate in which the likelihood of teaching by the Spirit is increased?

This final question gets at the heart of the most important thing we need to know about teaching and learning by the Spirit. Our final section will address that issue, and so we shall defer answering this question until then.

CHAPTER 14

CLARIFYING MISUNDERSTANDINGS

—————⇥•⇤—————

WELL INTENTIONED BUT NOT NECESSARILY ACCURATE

In chapter 4, we shared statements about teaching by the Spirit that have been made by various people. These illustrated that there are a number of misconceptions or misunderstandings about how the Spirit actually functions in teaching and learning settings. Some of these statements have elements of truth in them. Some can even be completely true at times, but if they are viewed as fixed rules or principles, they can be misleading.

Most of these statements were already clarified in the previous chapter as we answered common questions about what it means to teach by the Spirit. In this chapter we shall add only a few additional insights that will help us better understand the topic at hand.

If we are teaching by the Spirit, even small children will sit quietly.

I was present in the in-service training meeting where a stake

Primary president made this statement. It was a sweet promise made with sincere conviction. And I am sure that it is true in many cases. I have seen it happen myself. The problem is in stating it in such a sweeping, general way. My immediate reaction when I heard her statement was: If you happen to be in a ward where you have the last meeting in the block schedule and Primary goes until four in the afternoon, do restless, noisy, perhaps even unruly children prove that the teacher is out of tune with the Spirit? Or what about a troublemaker in a seminary or Sunday School class? Are they proof that the teacher is not fulfilling his or her calling? And I decided I would be particularly discouraged if I believed that if my own children didn't always sit quietly when I was trying to teach them, then I had failed in having the Spirit.

Two other statements from the list in chapter 4 are related to this idea.

- I think a good test for deciding whether I'm teaching by the Spirit is if my students like me and the class.
- If I come out of my lesson feeling discouraged or downhearted, then I know that I haven't taught by the Spirit.

There is no question that a powerful teaching moment may settle down even the unruly and nonattentive. It is also true that faithful and obedient learners will enjoy any experience where the teaching is being done with the influence of the Spirit. But if these statements are viewed as general principles about teaching by the Spirit, then what do we do with such situations as the following?

1. When Joseph taught his brothers what he had received in a dream, they plotted to kill him. They cast him into a pit, then sold him as a slave into Egypt (see Genesis 37:18–28).
2. After Jesus taught the people in His hometown of Nazareth, some of them were so incensed at what He said, they took

Him to the outskirts of the city and tried to throw Him off a cliff (see Luke 4:16–29).

3. I don't find many examples of Laman and Lemuel sitting quietly while being taught by either Lehi or Nephi.

4. Samuel the Lamanite's "class" ending up shooting at him with arrows and flinging rocks at him with their slings (see Helaman 16:2).

5. Abinadi's "students" burned him at the stake (see Mosiah 17).

The scriptures are full of such examples.

We had such a great class today. I felt the Spirit so strongly, I cried all the way through it.

See the discussion on pages 114–15 in the previous chapter.

I don't think it is right to use humor in our lessons because it is light-minded and actually offends the Spirit.

We are warned by the Lord to treat sacred things with reverence and care. They are not to be treated lightly. His counsel is very direct and oft repeated in that regard. "Remember that that which cometh from above is sacred, and must be spoken with care, and by constraint of the Spirit" (D&C 63:64). In another place we are warned against "idle thoughts," "excess of laughter," "light speeches" and "light-mindedness" (D&C 88:69, 121). Oliver Cowdery was told to "perform with soberness the work which I have commanded you" (D&C 6:35). We are counseled to be sober in many other places in the scriptures as well (see, for example, Mosiah 4:15; Alma 37:47; D&C 43:35). When speaking of the Sabbath day, the Lord used the phrase, "not with much laughter" (D&C 59:15).

But the Lord also said that we are to have "cheerful hearts and countenances" (D&C 59:15), and "Let thy heart be of good cheer before my face" (D&C 112:4). In fact, the phrase *good cheer* is found fourteen times in the standard works. To the pioneers about to cross the plains, the Lord said this: "If thou art merry, praise the Lord with singing, with music, with dancing, and with a prayer of praise and thanksgiving" (D&C 136:28).

We must always take care that we do not cross the line between having good, clean fun and being overly merry to the point of becoming irreverent. Sometimes jokes are shared that treat lightly sacred things or make fun of individuals or groups of people. I've seen this happen even in formal Church teaching settings such as sacrament meetings, firesides, and classrooms. I believe such things do offend the Spirit and cause it to withdraw to some degree.

There Comes a Point Where Laughter Changes in Nature

Here is an interesting observation by a colleague of mine, given one day when a group of us were discussing what the Lord meant by "loud laughter" or "light-mindedness." He used an experience in which he and his wife had come to ask themselves about this issue.

> My wife and I went out to dinner with a group of friends. There were eight or ten of us. After dinner, we went to one of the homes for dessert. As we sat around talking, a lot of funny things were said and we were all laughing. One couple shared an experience they had while courting that was hilarious. That triggered similar stories from other couples. It was in no way inappropriate and the spirit of friendship and good company was heightened by this shared companionship.
>
> But, human nature is such that when someone shares a funny story, others want to do the same. It's fun, and we want that pleasant experience to continue. That happened that night. As so often is the case, people feel like

123

they have to "top" the previous story. As that happened on this night, I began to notice a subtle change taking place. The laughter became louder and louder, more raucous, more forced. Someone shared a joke that was slightly off color. People laughed. It was quite funny, but I think we all sensed it was not appropriate. Then someone shared an experience that made fun of another person's peculiar habits.

Very quickly, the mood and atmosphere began to change. We were still having a good time, but there was this sense of unease, of laughing uproariously at things that really weren't that funny. Afterwards, on the way home, my wife and I tried to analyze what had happened. We concluded that maybe we had crossed the line somewhere and that maybe that was why the Lord warned us against "loud laughter."

Here are some words that might help us know when laughter and merriment become inappropriate: *flippant, irreverent, hurtful, demeaning, insulting, frivolous, profane, mocking, cruel, sarcastic,* or *contemptuous.*

Humor among the Brethren

On the other hand, there is surely what we might call a wholesome and healthy humor. Life itself provides more than its share of humorous, amusing situations. We can make wry observations that provoke laughter without demeaning others or treating sacred things lightly. One of the things that people loved most about President Gordon B. Hinckley was his very quick and dry wit and his delightful sense of humor. But it never crossed that line described above. He never joked about sacred things or demeaned anyone with his humor. Often, he poked gentle fun at himself.

Here is one example of his humor that I witnessed personally, which I believe actually helped to increase the Spirit in a meeting. While I was serving in Europe, President Hinckley came to England and held a regional conference for the Saints in all the British Isles. The conference was broadcast from the stake center in Preston, England. Preston was the center for some of the first missionary efforts in the Church outside of the United States. It was also the area where President Hinckley had served his mission many years before, so this was a homecoming of sorts for him. It was obvious that he was very glad to be there. Elder Harold C. Hillam was Area President at the time, and so he was responsible for all the arrangements. He also conducted the meeting.

When it came time for President Hinckley to speak, he reminisced about his missionary service in the area and then briefly spoke to the people in a near-perfect imitation of the heavy Lancashire accent prevalent there. The people were delighted and roared with laughter. A few minutes into his talk, he got a catch in his throat and stopped for a moment to try to clear it with a cough. President Hillam instantly jumped up and handed him a cup of water. After taking a sip, President Hinckley looked

There is a special gladness that goes with the gospel, and appropriate merriment. Yes, there is a mirth that can be heard among mortals who are estranged from the living God and from things as they really are. But it is a melancholy mirth. The jokes by drinkers about drunkenness are but an attempt to mock that which mocks them. Those who boast and chortle about their sexual conquests are boasting of that which has actually conquered them. The back room laughter of power brokers over the latest triumph is but contempt for those they say they serve; it is also the sound of impotence trying to reassure itself.

NEAL A. MAXWELL,
THINGS AS THEY REALLY ARE, XIV

at him and said, "President, is this your way of suggesting that my speech is too dry?"

Well, you can imagine how that was received. Laughter filled the hall. It was a wonderful moment of warmth and enjoyment. But I noticed something else. Those two moments added to the feelings of love and appreciation for our prophet. In that case, humor created a wonderful unity and readiness to be taught among us all.

We often see this in conference. President Thomas S. Monson has a wonderful sense of humor. Others of the First Presidency and the Twelve will make comments or share stories that fill the Conference Center with laughter. In fact, after each conference, when my grandchildren are asked to name what they remember from conference, they will often cite one of those humorous stories and the lesson they learned from it.

My friend and colleague was right to be concerned about overusing humor and being light-minded, but to say that humor is never appropriate would suggest that some of the best teachers in the Church are doing something wrong.

I didn't have time to prepare a lesson; I guess I'll have to teach by the Spirit today.

Here is another statement that contains truth but, if carried too far, becomes problematic. As we deal with this comment, let us also add in some of the other comments listed in chapter 4 that reflect the same basic misunderstanding. These include:

- I recently had a talk all prepared, but when I stood up, I felt impressed to put it aside and teach something entirely different, so now I'm wondering if I should prepare talks in advance.
- In my religion class we don't have prepared lessons. We have an opening prayer; then the teacher has us sit quietly and

wait for the Spirit to indicate what we should discuss that night.

- My companion and I tract "by the Spirit," meaning we walk down the street or sometimes just stop and wait for the Spirit to tell us where to go or what to do.

Unquestionably, there will be times when we have been asked to teach but then have circumstances unexpectedly come up that encroach on our preparation time. (The same situation may arise in family teaching settings as well.) In those circumstances, teachers or parents or priesthood leaders have the right to call on the Spirit to help them teach with power and effectiveness. But to extend that into a practice wherein one never prepares beforehand takes a true principle too far.

One of the principles that governs the giving and receiving of personal revelation is what I call "spiritual self-reliance."[1] Note carefully the Lord's strong language about this very concept:

> It is not meet that I should command in all things; for *he that is compelled in all things, the same is a slothful and not a wise servant;* . . . men should be anxiously engaged in a good cause, and do many things *of their own free will.* . . . They are agents unto themselves. . . . But he that doeth not anything until he is commanded, and receiveth a commandment with doubtful heart, and keepeth it with slothfulness, *the same is damned.* (D&C 58:26–29)

There is another principle here as well. We are not to try to force the things of the Spirit. Our privileges with the Spirit do not including determining what is given in revelation, when it comes, how it comes, or in what form it is given. Those are all controlled by the Spirit under the direction of the Father and the Son. So when a teacher tells the class that they will sit and wait for the

Spirit to direct them, that is a subtle way of trying to force the Spirit to operate on the teacher's timetable. The missionary who stands and waits to be told where to go and which doors to knock on is doing the same thing.

Elder Neal A. Maxwell said this about deliberately not preparing to teach:

> Teaching does not remove responsibility from the teacher for prayerful and pondering preparation. Teaching by the Spirit is not the equivalent of going on "automatic pilot." We still need a carefully worked out flight plan. Studying out something in our own minds involves the Spirit in our preparations as well as in our presentations. We must not err, like Oliver Cowdery, by taking no thought except to ask God for his Spirit (see D&C 9:7).[2]

We should recognize that the Lord will speak to us through the Spirit in his own time and in his own way. Many people do not understand this principle. They believe that when they are ready and when it suits their convenience, they can call upon the Lord and he will immediately respond, even in the precise way they have prescribed.

DALLIN H. OAKS,
"TEACHING AND LEARNING BY THE SPIRIT," 10

I'm not interested in all these teaching methods; I just want to teach by the Spirit.

This is a little more complicated question. When it comes to teaching methodology and teaching skills and abilities, there are cautions as well as encouragements. One of those cautions is clearly related to what we just said about "forcing" the Spirit. If the above statement reflects an attitude similar to that of the teacher and missionary who wanted the Spirit to do it all for them, then it is not a wise statement. In other words, the teacher here might be saying, "If I'm teaching by the Spirit, then I don't have to worry about how I teach. That will take care of itself." I think we have shown that such an attitude is not pleasing to the Lord.

On the other hand, that statement may reflect a desire to trust in the Spirit more than in the methodologies and wisdom of men. The Lord's warning in section 50 of the Doctrine and Covenants is sobering. If we preach in any way other than by the Spirit of truth, it is not of God. With that scripture in mind, Elder Dallin H. Oaks made this observation:

> If we rely on debate techniques or sales methods or group psychology, we are preaching the gospel in some other way, and it is not of God. We must teach the gospel by the Spirit, and we must testify to the truth. When this is done, the Holy Spirit will testify to the sincere seeker that the things that have been said are true. Intellectual things—reason and logic—can prepare the way, and they can help us in our preparation. But if we are tied to them instead of to the Spirit of the Lord, we are not teaching the gospel in the Lord's way.[3]

But does "any other way" exclude any focus on teaching skills or methods that have been proven to help enhance learner readiness, learner participation, or application of learning? Remember that in chapter 12, we discussed how the Holy Ghost can increase our skills and abilities in many fields of endeavor. Couldn't that be true in teaching? One of the gifts of the Spirit is the gift of teaching. Obviously, it can't be wrong to pray for that gift for those of us who teach as parents or in a profession or a Church calling. But right alongside that discussion we included a quote by Elder

Maxwell in which he talked about teachers who lack "teaching charisma" but who still teach with the power of the Spirit.

So where is the balance? Is it possible that an individual's readiness to learn can be lessened by a dull, boring, monotonous, or lifeless presentation? If a teacher uses a variety of effective methods that engage the learners and help draw them into the learning experience, couldn't this actually enhance the opportunity for the Spirit to function?

Shortly after the new missionary study guide, *Preach My Gospel,* came out, Elder Richard G. Scott spoke about it in general conference. Among other things, he said:

> *Preach My Gospel* contains chapters that give extremely valuable information on how to recognize and understand the guidance of the Holy Spirit. There are scriptures on how to effectively study and *how to refine personal teaching skills.* . . . Using the inspired content of *Preach My Gospel,* many missionaries have made dramatic improvements in their capacity to teach with conviction and to invite the confirming witness of the Holy Ghost. Recently I asked two assistants to a mission president to share the vision of Joseph Smith while I acted as the investigator. I planned to vigorously challenge them to see how they would respond. Yet the sincerity of their message, the purity of their intent, *the skill with which it was delivered,* even in a practice session, was so compelling that I could not do it.[4]

That certainly makes it clear that seeking to improve our ability to teach the gospel more skillfully is not displeasing to the Lord. But we have a more powerful example than that. Wasn't Jesus an example of masterful teaching? And look at how many different methods He used in addition to preaching and proclaiming the gospel. He told stories. He constantly drew on everyday objects to illustrate points. He asked questions. He challenged traditional ways of seeing things. He taught from the scriptures.

Of course there are cautions. Here are just a few: There is danger if a teacher comes to believe that methods are *the* answer to more powerful teaching. Skills are desirable, but they do not take priority over teaching by the Spirit. There is danger if a teacher begins to think gimmicks and games, gadgets and toys, cleverness and entertainment are the things that constitute good teaching. Of this last item, speaking to teachers in the Church Educational System, Elder Richard G. Scott said:

> Those of you who are beginning service as an instrument in the hands of the Lord in teaching and testifying to the youth of the Church will learn an important lesson that the more experienced have long since confirmed. There is no place in your teaching for gimmicks, fads, or bribery by favors or treats. Such activities produce no lasting motivator for personal growth nor any enduring beneficial results. Simply stated, truths presented in an environment of true love and trust qualify for the confirming witness of the Holy Spirit.[5]

We have already mentioned the new curriculum for youth that was introduced throughout the Church beginning in 2013. In support of that and other curriculum materials, the Church has also posted helps for teaching. Here is some excellent counsel from those materials:

> No teacher should fall into a monotonous pattern of presenting the same kind of lesson week after week. When you teach with variety, learners tend to understand gospel principles better and retain more. As you strive to choose

effective teaching methods, ask yourself: Will the method invite the Spirit? Will the method help learners better understand the gospel principle? Will the method invite students to participate in the lesson? Will the method make the best use of time? It is important to begin your lesson in a way that prepares others to learn. You can do such things as present an object lesson, write questions on the board, or have someone read a story or scripture. It is also important to conclude your lesson in a way that invites learners to live what they have learned. You can review the main principles taught and ask learners how to apply them, ask an individual to summarize the main points of the lesson, and bear testimony of the principles.[6]

Summary

We have attempted to answer the questions, and we have attempted to respond to the various statements we often hear. In the end, this is all that matters:

"That which doth not edify is not of God, and is darkness" (D&C 50:23).

CHAPTER 15

SOME WORDS OF CAUTION

OCCUPATIONAL HAZARDS

For many years, the Church Educational System has sponsored a program for its teachers and staff, both paid employees and volunteers, called "An Evening with . . ." For each event, the name of the invited speaker is inserted: for example, "An Evening with President Spencer W. Kimball," or "An Evening with Elder Russell M. Nelson." The speakers are usually drawn from the First Presidency or the Quorum of the Twelve.

In 1978, Elder Jeffrey R. Holland, who was then serving as Commissioner of the Church Educational System (CES), introduced Elder Gordon B. Hinckley as part of that series. In his introductory remarks, Elder Holland told about working on a construction crew during the summers while he was in college. He spoke of the hazards found in that work and how his employers posted warning signs and set up safety requirements to help keep them safe. He then said:

Our own occupation has unique hazards, if I may call them that, and our employers have some of that same loving concern. . . . They are, like the signs on the shack where the blasting powder is kept, a reminder. They are always there—for our good—and I suppose that they must always be there.[1]

He then said that in his position as Commissioner, he had been asked by the Brethren who oversee CES to speak to the group that night about one such hazard that was a concern to them. (More on what that hazard was will be shared later.)

I like that analogy. There are "occupational hazards" associated with our teaching. We have to accept the fact that Satan will try to get his hands into the process of teaching because it is so central to God's work. Some of his ploys are very subtle, even seductive. And one scripture points several such hazards out clearly and plainly for us. The scripture I refer to comes from the writings of Nephi. I hesitate to explore it here because in some ways it is quite a negative take on one aspect of teaching. But I believe Nephi was inspired to include it in his record for our day.

"THERE SHALL BE NO PRIESTCRAFTS"

The word *priestcraft* (including its plural, *priestcrafts*) is found eight times in scripture. All but one of those are in the Book of Mormon.[2] Jacob prophesied that Jesus would be crucified because of priestcraft (see 2 Nephi 10:5). Alma accused Nehor of introducing priestcraft into the Nephite Church and trying to enforce it with the sword (see Alma 1:12, 16). During His visit to the Americas, Jesus spoke of priestcrafts three different times (see 3 Nephi 16:10; 21:19; 30:2).

The word *craft* generally refers to a trade or an occupation that requires a unique set of knowledge, skills, and abilities. These are acquired through extensive training and experience. A craftsman is one who possesses those kinds of skills and experience. To link *priest* and *craft* together would therefore suggest a person who has been taught and trained in the duties of a leader of a church or religious congregation. There is an implication that this is the person's occupation or profession, and therefore the source of his or her livelihood.

In the Book of Mormon, the word carries a strong pejorative, or negative, connotation. From what is said, priestcraft in Book

The sin of priestcraft is a grievous one. Time after time the Lord has condemned those who appear to men to be his servants, but who, though they draw near to him with their lips, have removed their hearts far from him. . . . In modern as in ancient times, those who appear to be servants of the Lord and present themselves to labor in his vineyard are subject to the prophetic principle: "The laborer in Zion shall labor for Zion; for if they labor for money they shall perish" (2 Nephi 26:31).

DALLIN H. OAKS,
PURE IN HEART, 17

of Mormon times involved people who set themselves up as religious leaders in opposition to and outside of the Church set up by Christ. "False priests" or "apostate priests" might be good synonyms for someone practicing priestcraft.

"But wait," you may be saying, "what does priestcraft have to do with teaching by the Spirit? Is it really a problem?" To answer those questions, let me ask and answer another question.

Do we really have priestcraft in today's Church? If by that question we mean, "Is priestcraft a common problem?" I would say no, not in the same way it was in the Book of Mormon. But from the earliest days of the Restoration to the present, there have been members who have felt that they had greater light and knowledge than those called by God to lead the Church. They publicly preached against those leaders and convinced numerous others to follow them. In several cases, they eventually broke off and started new churches. Sometimes they were so bitter that they actually cooperated with enemies of the Church who were persecuting the Saints.

Most of that has died out as we moved on. But although we may see it rarely today, priestcraft still does occur. In recent years one such church that was formed by former members of our Church has made national news, often causing others to link their church with ours. But I believe we see some of the milder forms of priestcraft, if that is an appropriate way to describe them, happening frequently enough that it is a concern. Any time it occurs, in any form, people are misled and confused, and the work is hampered to some degree.

"Priestcrafts Are That . . ."

We did not include Nephi's reference in our summary above. Let us look at that verse now, for it doesn't just mention priestcraft, it *defines* it! And it is in his definition that we find the danger signs posted. In the closing chapters of his record, Nephi prophesied at length about the last days (see 2 Nephi 26:14). Here is one thing he wrote:

> [The Lord] commandeth that there shall be no priestcrafts; for, behold, priestcrafts are that men preach and set themselves up for a light unto the world, that they may get gain and praise of the world; but they seek not the welfare of Zion. (2 Nephi 26:29)

Nephi defines *priestcraft* with four attributes or behaviors:

- *It involves preaching.* We are not talking about academic, professional, or business occupations. The word *priest* implies the connection to religion, but Nephi confirms it. The occupation of a priest is to preach—and remember, the word *preach* means to declare the good news of God's plan and Christ's Atonement.

- *They set themselves up as "a" light to the world.* This is in contrast to Christ, who is "*the* light of the world" (John 9:5; 3 Nephi 11:11). In the scriptures, light is associated with spirit, intelligence, and truth (see D&C 93:36).
- *They seek gain and the praise of the world.* This is what motivates them. Gain and praise could include power, position, fame, popularity, glory, prestige, and influence as well as monetary gain.
- *They seek not the welfare of Zion.* They do not strive to build up the kingdom of God and further God's purposes for His children. Their hearts are set elsewhere.

Please note that the last three of these descriptors, even in their less virulent forms, are all things that offend and grieve the Spirit. This is why a discussion of priestcraft is directly relevant to our discussion of teaching by the Spirit. So let's take those last three points one at a time.

Setting Ourselves Up as a Light

There are people who believe that their knowledge or understanding is superior to that of those called and ordained to lead the Church. Such people create a serious breach between themselves and the Spirit with this particularly egregious form of pride. To be proud and puffed up about personal attributes or accomplishments—being more beautiful, more intelligent, more "gifted" than others—is a form of spiritual nearsightedness. But to believe that we know more than God, more than His prophets, seers, and revelators? That can be especially deadly to one's spiritual sensitivity.

Let us go back now to the "hazard" that Elder Holland was asked by the Brethren to discuss with the seminary and institute teachers who were present that night in 1978.

> Brethren and sisters, please be cautious and restrained and totally orthodox in all matters of Church doctrine. This is, as you might suppose, of great concern to the Brethren. . . . They cannot fail to respond to some anxiety expressed by a member of the Church who feels that some inappropriate doctrinal or historical position has been taken in the classroom.[3]

Though given to professional teachers who were paid employees and not ministers, that counsel has application for all who would teach the gospel. For example, how many times have we sat in a Sunday School class or a priesthood quorum when the called teachers set aside the prepared, approved curriculum to teach what they deemed to be something of "greater value." Sometimes they are openly critical of Church leaders or Church policy. Sometimes they share some sensational interpretation of doctrine or some story that raises doubts rather than strengthens faith. These are not evil people out to destroy the Church. In many cases, they really believe that what they are doing is of greater value to their listeners than teaching from the scriptures or prepared curriculum. But isn't that what Nephi meant when he said that they "set *themselves* up" as the light?

We need to do a more thorough job in the teaching process to get the Spirit down into the hearts of the people. It is more than intellectual, it is more than a mental assessment. It must be a thing of the heart, a thing of the Spirit.

GORDON B. HINCKLEY,
TEACHINGS, 619

Many years ago, while I was serving as bishop, one of our ward members brought me a cassette tape recording of a fireside he had recently attended. He said it was pretty exciting stuff, but he wanted to see what I thought of it. The opening line by the speaker went something like this. "You are going to hear things tonight that you don't hear commonly taught by the First Presidency or the Quorum of the Twelve. That's because those wonderful Brethren are so busy with their callings, they don't have the time to study the scriptures like I do."

The amazing thing to me was that the person who gave me the recording hadn't seen that statement as a wildly waving red flag.

> *Doctrinal interpretation is the province of the First Presidency. The Lord has given that stewardship to them by revelation. No teacher has the right to interpret doctrine for the members of the Church.*
>
> EZRA TAFT BENSON,
> *TEACHINGS,* 317

I listened to only a small part of the recording, but that was all I needed to see that this was a form of priestcraft. Not only was this man interpreting doctrine and teaching principles that went beyond what has been taught by ordained Church leaders, but he was also clearly glorying in his role as teacher and revelator. He loved the sensation he was creating. Later I learned that he was warned by his stake president to cease teaching those things or face Church disciplinary action. He complied.

Seeking Gain and the Praise of the World Rather Than the Building Up of Zion

Part of priestcraft is the desire for worldly gain in all of its forms. Unfortunately, there always seem to be those who are willing to pay for "preaching" that pleases them. When Nehor preached false doctrine to the people, "they began to support him and give him money" (Alma 1:5). Moroni prophesied that in the last days, some churches would say: "Come unto me, and for your money you shall be forgiven of your sins" (Mormon 8:32). Samuel the Lamanite said that the very ones who rejected the prophets would give false prophets gold and silver and clothe them in costly apparel (see Helaman 13:28).

If you think of *gain* only in terms of actual money, then I don't think we see much priestcraft in the Church today.[4] But if you add in the desire for the praise of the world, or when a person is seeking something other than the welfare of Zion, then I believe we have a subtle but nevertheless real form of priestcraft. We don't have to be "priests" by profession to be guilty of priestcraft. For example, the desire to be liked by one's students—or children or ward members—is a natural thing, but we must be careful that we don't let a desire for the praise of the world become a driving determinant of what we teach and how we teach it.

When I was a young seminary teacher, I had a wise old principal named Wally Montague. As we were talking about teaching one day, he made this observation:

> It has been my experience that we who teach for a living have to be very careful. There is an inherent danger in our profession, and that is that when we teach well, it is only natural that our students begin to praise us. "Oh, I loved your class today, Brother Montague." "You are such a great teacher, Brother Montague."

"Who doesn't want to be a good teacher?" I thought. "Is that so bad?" He must have guessed what I was thinking, because he then said this:

> Here is the danger. And the more you achieve excellence in your teaching, the greater is the likelihood that this will happen. You finish a particularly fine class one

day. Everything goes superbly. You could tell you really connected with the students, and you even felt the Spirit was there strongly at times. As the class ends, a student comes up to you and says, "Oh, Brother Lund, you were absolutely wonderful today. It was one of the best lessons ever." If you are not careful, you may find yourself inwardly thinking, "Yeah, it really was pretty terrific."

I saw immediately why he had called it a danger. I guess it hit home because I had, not many days previously, had something very much like that occur after one of my classes. "So, how do you guard against that?" I asked. "It seems like it's a pretty easy thing to get caught up in." His answer touched me deeply, and I still remember it with great clarity even after all these years.

I've added three things to my daily prayers, especially those prayers I offer just before class. They are, first: "Father in Heaven, I thank Thee for the privilege of teaching Thy children. Help me to do and say only those things which are pleasing to Thee and to Thy Spirit." Second: "Father, I thank Thee for what gifts Thou hast given me. I acknowledge that these are gifts from Thee

You do not have to sneak up behind this spiritually experienced youth and whisper religion in his ears; you can come right out, face to face, and talk with him. You do not need to disguise religious truths with a cloak of worldly things; you can bring these truths to him openly, in their natural guise. Youth may prove to be not more fearful of them than you are. There is no need for gradual approaches, for "bedtime" stories, for coddling, for patronizing, or for any of the other childish devices used in efforts to reach those spiritually inexperienced and all but spiritually dead.

J. REUBEN CLARK JR.,
THE CHARTED COURSE

and not just the product of my own efforts." And finally, I loosely quote a verse from the Sermon on the Mount. I say, "Help me, O Lord, to let *my* light so shine before these students, so that as they see *my* good works, they will be led to glorify *Thee,* O our Father who art in heaven" [see Matthew 5:16].

That wise and gentle counsel has made a great deal of difference to me over the years. I strongly believe that Nephi was inspired to define *priestcraft* when he mentioned it so that we in the latter-day Church would see the dangers that can so subtly creep into our teaching.

CHAPTER 16

"Nourished by the Good Word of God"

———⸙———

Teaching and Nourishing

In his final writings in the Book of Mormon record, Moroni added one short chapter in which he described how the Church of Jesus Christ functioned in his time. It is a brief but quite remarkable account showing what the Church is like when it is functioning properly. His counsel is particularly relevant for our discussion on teaching by the Spirit.

> Their meetings were conducted by the church *after the manner of the workings of the Spirit,* and by the power of the Holy Ghost; for as the power of the Holy Ghost led them whether to preach, or to exhort, or to pray, or to supplicate, or to sing, even so it was done. (Moroni 6:9)

What a remarkable standard for us today! Wouldn't it be wonderful if every ward, every branch, every mission, every stake, every district, could say that of their own efforts and actions.

What I find especially interesting about that statement is what precedes it. In the earlier verses of that chapter, Moroni describes the things that they did in the Church at that time—and how they did them—that resulted in that level of spirituality. One of the things he listed is particularly noteworthy in our discussion here.

> And after they had been received unto baptism, and were wrought upon and cleansed by the power of the Holy Ghost, they were numbered among the people of the church of Christ; and their names were taken, *that they might be remembered and nourished by the good word of God,* to keep them in the right way. (Moroni 6:4)

There it is, in simple and clear terms. They nourished their people with the word of God. That brings us back to what we said in chapter 1: One of the major functions and obligations of the Church of Jesus Christ is to preach and teach the gospel by the Spirit. We are not just Church leaders and Church members, we are gospel teachers. And we are not just called to teach. We are to teach so that souls are nourished, faith is strengthened, and conversion is deepened.

What a wonderful way to describe how the Church is to minister to its members! President Gordon B. Hinckley made reference to Moroni's counsel in one of his best-known teachings. He said: "Every one . . . needs three things: a friend, a responsibility, and nurturing

Every member of The Church of Jesus Christ of Latter-day Saints is, or will be, a teacher. Each of us has a vital interest in the content and effectiveness of gospel teaching. We want everyone to have great gospel teachers, and we want those teachers to help all of us find our way back, not just to them but to our Heavenly Father.

DALLIN H. OAKS,
"GOSPEL TEACHING," 78

with 'the good word of God.' It is our duty and opportunity to provide these things."[1]

Two years following President Hinckley's statement, Elder Dallin H. Oaks said this about gospel teaching in the Church:

> Several years ago the First Presidency challenged the Quorum of the Twelve to revitalize teaching in the Church. The Twelve, assisted by the Seventy, accepted that challenge. Now, after years of preparation, engaging the efforts of superb gospel teachers, scholars, writers, and others, the First Presidency has just sent a letter launching a Church-wide effort "to revitalize and improve teaching in the Church." This letter states, "This renewed emphasis is intended to improve gospel teaching in homes and in Church meetings and help nourish members with the good word of God."[2]

The choice of the verb *revitalize* is interesting. Perhaps part of the reason for that comes from an observation made some years earlier by President Spencer W. Kimball:

> I fear that all too often many of our members come to church, sit through a class or a meeting, and . . . then return home having been largely [uninspired]. It is especially unfortunate when this happens at a time . . . of stress, temptation, or crisis. We all need to be touched and nurtured by the Spirit, and *effective teaching* is one of the most important ways this can happen."[3]

That effort to strengthen teaching in the Church continues to this day. We have already noted current efforts to produce curriculum and teaching support materials directly aimed at helping members teach and learn more consistently by the Spirit.

In harmony with those efforts, I would like to suggest four simple and practical things we can do to enhance the quality of our teaching. I strongly believe these will enhance the teaching climate in a way that invites the Spirit to be present. If that happens, then those we teach will not, as President Kimball suggested, go away uninspired.

Although these suggestions are couched in terms of more formal classroom settings, there can be direct application of some of them in other teaching settings such as family home evenings, ward and stake council meetings, leadership training, and other meetings where formal, interactive teaching takes place.

FOUR WAYS WE CAN BETTER HELP NURTURE OTHERS AS WE TEACH

Principle 1: Prepare Carefully and Well

An important part of teaching *by* the Spirit is preparing *with* the Spirit. Poor teaching is very often the result of poor or inadequate preparation. We have already noted that there are times when the Spirit may prompt us to leave a prepared lesson or talk to teach something else. But in the vast majority of cases, we have time to prepare what we are going to say, then deliver it with the help of the Spirit.

It is disappointing to hear of teachers who don't even look at their lesson manuals until an hour or two before they are to teach. Occasionally we even see teachers preparing their lessons during sacrament meeting to be delivered immediately thereafter. Perhaps, from time to time, there may have been urgencies at home that left them little or no time to prepare, but I think we can safely say that far too often it is because preparing well is not seen as a high priority. They are satisfied with "getting by."

It has been my experience that when we take the time to look at our next lesson a few days or even a week in advance, a remarkable thing happens. During the days leading up to the teaching time, the Spirit often brings things to our attention and remembrance that will enhance our lesson or our teaching methods. We see or hear something and think, "Oh, that will be perfect for my lesson on Sunday."

Part of good teaching is deciding not only *what* to teach but *how* to teach it. In addition to outlining the key points—doctrine, principles, or concepts—of the lesson, we must also decide how these can be most effectively taught. Will we use a good story to illustrate a principle? Outline it on the board? Allow the students to discuss it in small groups together? Lead the learners through a scriptural chain? Give them a worksheet or study guide? Good teaching is not just content preparation, but method preparation as well.

Good teachers also teach both for *understanding* and for *application.* They teach a gospel principle and then encourage their listeners to discuss how that principle directly applies to them or those they love. Nephi called this "likening" the scriptures unto ourselves (see 1 Nephi 19:23). If the doctrine and principles do not change how we live—strengthen faith, cause us to repent, or give us a greater desire to serve—then we have not finished the gospel learning process. Remember James's wise counsel: "Be ye doers of the word, and not hearers only, deceiving yourselves" (James 1:22).

However, let me add one caution that I have learned from my own experience. If we teach the doctrine and principles clearly and with power, the Holy Ghost often helps individuals to make personal application without us having to spell it out for them in every detail. It is much more powerful when they discover these things for themselves with the help of the Holy Ghost.

The new youth curriculum suggests that teachers encourage

students to share their feelings and what they have learned with each other. That is another excellent way to help individuals liken the scriptures unto themselves. Therefore, a wise teacher or parent gives careful thought when preparing lessons and talks as to how he or she can help to facilitate the "likening" process.

While we are talking about preparation, let me suggest one other caution. In cases where we are called to teach from prepared manuals or other materials furnished by the Church, we are expected to use those materials as the source of what we teach. As noted earlier, it is tempting to think that what we have is better or more interesting or more relevant to our students than what we are asked to teach. Such feelings border on priestcraft, which very quickly can grieve the Spirit.

> *I have sometimes observed teachers who gave the designated chapter no more than a casual mention and then presented a lesson and invited discussion on other materials of the teacher's choice. That is not acceptable. A gospel teacher is not called to choose the subject of the lesson but to teach and discuss what has been specified. Gospel teachers should also be scrupulous to avoid hobby topics, personal speculations, and controversial subjects.*
>
> DALLIN H. OAKS,
> "GOSPEL TEACHING," 80

Principle 2: Encourage the Learners to Actively Participate in the Learning Process

In the scriptures we are told that we must learn not just by *study,* but also by *faith* (see D&C 88:118; 109:7, 14). We know that "faith is a principle of action,"[4] so learning by faith clearly requires some kind of action on our part. When we actively participate in the teaching and learning experience, it increases our opportunities to learn by faith. And such participation helps bring the Spirit into the teaching and learning setting. Therefore, teachers should make a special effort to do more than be just a "talking head" to their students or their children. (This of course would not apply in formal meetings such as sacrament meeting or conferences.)

Elder Richard G. Scott made this interesting observation:

> When you encourage students to raise their hand to respond to a question, they will signify to the Holy Spirit their willingness to learn. That use of moral agency will allow the Spirit to motivate and give them more powerful guidance during your time together. *Participation allows individuals to experience being led by the Spirit.*[5]

Some forms of class participation are more effective in encouraging learning, and therefore in bringing the Spirit, than others. Sometimes teachers feel like they have to entertain younger children by playing various games. Some instructional games can be useful and certainly get students participating, but if one is not careful, learning is sacrificed for fun and the Spirit may withdraw.

Our purpose here is not to discuss various teaching methods, but I would like to note one thing we can do that is particularly helpful in bringing the Spirit into a gospel learning setting. And this is as true in settings like family home evening as it is in formal classrooms. Alma taught that the word has a more powerful effect on the mind than the sword or anything else. The scripture says, "Therefore Alma thought it was expedient that they should try the virtue of the word of God" (Alma 31:5). It is my conviction that Alma speaks literally here and not just metaphorically. There is real power in the word, especially as it is found in the scriptures.

Therefore, as teachers, if we can get our students to become actively engaged in studying the scriptures, even in formal teaching settings, we can facilitate that power coming into their lives. Here are some practical ways to do that:

- Encourage every individual to have his or her own personal copy of the scriptures.
- Don't just read passages to them. Have them open the scriptures and follow along. Have them read aloud some of the time.
- Give them page numbers so they can easily find the reference, and be sure you wait until everyone is there so they can follow with you.
- Encourage them to use the study aids in the LDS edition of the scriptures. Point out helps and insights found in footnotes, chapter summaries, cross-references, word definitions, and so on.
- Point significant things out to them, such as patterns, relationships, a word that isn't clear, something of particular importance that they may overlook.
- Encourage them to mark their scriptures. This is another form of active participation. This can be done by simply saying things like, "This verse is important. You may want to mark it," or, "I wrote this cross-reference in the margin of my scriptures."
- Send them into the scriptures looking for things. We do this by asking meaningful questions that lead them to discover things on their own. For example: "Why did the Savior compare Himself to living water to the Samaritan woman at the well?" "Why did the Lord wait until Lehi's family were several days into the wilderness before telling Lehi to send his sons back for the brass plates?" "How does verse 67 in D&C 10 help clarify verse 55?"

- As part of that effort, ask "likening" or "application" questions such as, "Why did Mormon break his historical narrative about Korihor to make a 'thus we see' comment?" (see Alma 30:60). "What can we learn about how personal revelation may come from how Oliver Cowdery got his testimony that Joseph Smith was a prophet?" (see D&C 6:15–24).

A teacher can do much to encourage active participation by helping the learner become engaged in the learning experience. Obviously, the suggestions above are applicable where a teacher (be it a parent, priesthood or auxiliary leader, or formal classroom instructor) has an opportunity to interact with a relatively small group of learners. In other cases, the techniques might not be appropriate. For example, speakers in sacrament meeting are encouraged *not* to ask the congregation to follow along in their own scriptures, as this may actually be disruptive of the reverent spirit we expect in sacrament meetings. With that said, however, we often find effective teachers adapting the above techniques for large groups. For example, they ask those same kinds of thought-provoking questions of the audience to stimulate thinking, even though they don't expect anyone to actually answer.

"This Is Not Going to Be Pretty"

Some years ago, the seminaries and institutes of religion introduced a new focus in their curriculum called "sequential scripture teaching." In essence, it was a change from "concept teaching," that is, having each lesson focus on a gospel topic supported by a few scriptural references and lots of stories, worksheets, instructional games, and so on. In this new approach, the focus was on teaching blocks of scripture as they appear sequentially in the standard works. For example, you teach 1 Nephi, then 2 Nephi, then Jacob, and so on.

As part of our efforts to implement this emphasis, several of us traveled to the Midwest to observe early-morning seminary teachers and see how they were doing with this new approach. I was assigned to observe a teacher in Oklahoma. We arrived about 6:15 a.m. and watched the teacher, whom I will call Sister Jones, greet her students as they came in—or in some cases, stumbled in. This teacher was an older woman, probably in her mid-sixties. She was tiny, only a little more than five feet tall, and probably weighed barely a hundred pounds. She was also very soft-spoken. She had fifteen or so students, including several very husky, football-player type boys who were laughing and talking as they arrived. As I watched them file in, I thought to myself, "Oh my, this is not going to be pretty."

I was wrong. What followed was a remarkable experience. The first thing that became very obvious was that she loved these kids, and they loved her. But it was more than that. Every student had scriptures on his or her desk. Sister Jones didn't just talk *about* the scriptures. She didn't just teach *with* the scriptures. She taught *from* the scriptures. She made sure all the students had their scriptures open and were following along. She led them into the scriptures with the very techniques noted above. She asked questions. She sent them looking for things. She had them cross-referencing. She asked them to comment on what they thought a passage meant. It was an inspiring experience for me personally. I opened my scriptures and for a time forgot I was there as an observer.

Afterwards, as the class was breaking up, I went up to a couple of those husky guys and struck up a conversation. "So, do you enjoy seminary?" I said.

"Oh, yes," they said in chorus. "We love seminary."

Then one of the boys, who towered above me and probably

outweighed Sister Jones by two hundred pounds, actually got a little misty-eyed. "Sister Jones is awesome," he said. "She is way cool."

"And why do you say that?" I asked, expecting him to say something about how much she loved them.

But his answer was even better than that. "Because she helped me gain a testimony," he said softly.

Principle 3: Know Your Students

Here, too, we are speaking of smaller class-type settings. Obviously a speaker in stake conference isn't going to teach like he or she would in a classroom. But in settings where the teacher and his or her learners get together on a regular basis, it is so important to come to know each individual. It is a way of showing individuals that they are important to us, that we care about them.

It is also so much easier to encourage learner participation if we can call on individuals by name. And wherever possible, "knowing" means much more than just knowing their names. The more you know about the learners, the more you can direct questions and discussion to those who may need it most or who have a special contribution to make.

The calling of the gospel teacher is one of the noblest in the world. The good teacher can make all the difference in inspiring boys and girls and men and women to change their lives and fulfill their highest destiny. The importance of the teacher has been beautifully described by Daniel Webster when he said, "If we work upon marble, it will perish; if we work upon brass, time will efface it; but if we work upon immortal minds, if we imbue them with principles and the just fear of God and love of our fellowman, we engrave upon those tablets something that will brighten through all eternity."

Harold B. Lee,
Teachings, 461

We could give numerous examples of how that works, but I think the concept is self-evident. When you think about it, isn't that what Moroni meant when he said of new converts: "And their names were taken" (Moroni 6:4)?

Principle 4. Focus Primarily on Doctrine and Principles, Then Testify of Their Truthfulness

President Boyd K. Packer has said:

> True doctrine, understood, changes attitudes and behaviors. The study of the doctrines of the gospel will improve behavior quicker than a study of behavior will improve behavior. . . . That is why we stress so forcefully the study of the doctrines of the gospel.[6]

Alma resigned the chief judgeship so that "he himself might go forth among his people, . . . that he might preach the word of God unto them, to stir them up in remembrance of their duty, and that he might pull down, by the word of God, all the pride and craftiness and all the contentions which were among his people, *seeing no way that he might reclaim them save it were in bearing down in pure testimony*" (Alma 4:19).

It is in the doctrine and principles of the gospel that we find the power to soften hearts, to change lives, to bring souls to repentance. I believe Satan fully understands this and tries to tempt teachers to stay away from the "boring stuff" because they think it will be too much for the students. In fact, just the opposite may be true.

Let me go back to that time when seminaries and institutes went to a scripture-based curriculum. When the new plan was first announced, we immediately got a lot of push back, especially from teachers who taught students five days a week. It would never work, they said. Students would quickly get bored, and bored

154

students were a recipe for disciplinary problems. "Half of teaching is entertainment," one teacher said. "If they're not having fun, you've got problems."

Then he added, "Teenagers are like hungry tigers. You either feed them and keep them at bay, or they'll eat you alive."

We didn't believe that. We believed what President J. Reuben Clark Jr. said about our youth being spiritually mature, that they didn't need to be coddled or played with, that we didn't need to sneak up on them and whisper the gospel in their ears (see inset box on page 141 of chapter 15). And we also believed what Alma said, that there is power in the word of God. One of our Church Educational System leaders, after hearing the tiger comment, wryly observed, "In a way, it's true about teenagers being hungry, but the best way to satisfy a hungry tiger is to feed it meat and not milk."

As the program unfolded, something amazing began to happen. Over and over, reports started coming in from teachers all over the world—full-time and part-time, those with long experience and those who were new to the classroom. They told us that when they were in the scriptures—not just reading them *at* their students, but leading the students into the scriptures, having them actively engaged in the study process—*their disciplinary problems actually went down!*

Alma taught his son Helaman that "by small and simple things are great things brought to pass; and small means in many instances doth confound the wise" (Alma 37:6). These four principles of teaching are small and simple, but I can tell you from my own personal experience, and from the testimony of many other wonderful teachers, that they work. And by *working,* what we mean is this: Preparing well, knowing your students, and keeping them actively engaged in the learning experience, especially by focusing on the scriptures and true doctrine, brings the Spirit into the teaching setting, and the Holy Ghost begins to fulfill His functions with both teacher and learner. Put simply, teaching and learning by the Spirit will occur.

Let us remember Moroni's wise observation about how the early Church worked in his time to strengthen members: "And their names were taken, *that they might be remembered and nourished by the good word of God,* to keep them in the right way" (Moroni 6:4).

PART IV

MORE IN TUNE

CHAPTER 17

PUTTING OURSELVES IN TUNE— DRAWING CLOSER TO THE SPIRIT

—+>•<+—

KEYS TO HAVING THE SPIRIT WHILE WE TEACH, PREACH, COUNSEL, AND LEAD

The Lord said in unequivocal language: "If ye receive not the Spirit ye shall not teach" (D&C 42:14). A short time later He warned that if we preach in some other way than with the Spirit of truth, "it is not of God" (D&C 50:18).

That is our clear and powerful charge. So let us now conclude with the most important key of all the questions we could ask about teaching by the Spirit:

What can we do as individuals to ensure that we will have the Spirit whenever and wherever we teach the gospel so that we in no way offend the Holy Ghost, and so that both we and those we teach are edified?

Before answering that question, a quick reminder is in order. As noted in chapter 2, the Holy Ghost is a member of the Godhead, and as such He plays a major role in our journey toward eternal life. We cannot stay on that path without His counsel, direction, warnings, enlightenment, and comfort. We cannot stress that strongly enough. Though we often talk about becoming more like Christ and more like our Father in Heaven, we don't always remind ourselves that this is done only with the help of the Spirit. And one of the major functions of the Holy Ghost in His role as Divine Teacher is to participate in the teaching and learning process in partnership with us finite and imperfect mortals.

Much of what we have been given in the scriptures and the teachings of living prophets is directly aimed at helping us draw close to the Spirit, because that is the key to gaining eternal life. These are the fundamentals of the gospel—faith, repentance, humility, prayer, service, covenants, temple worship, scriptures, and so forth. So if our question was, "How do we draw closer to the Spirit?" those would be a major focus of our answer.

But in this book, we are focusing on the role of the Holy Ghost as teacher and guide, mentor and enlightener, testifier and confirmer. So our focus in this chapter is to look at things that specifically aid us in our quest to have the Holy Ghost as our companion in teaching and learning settings. That we do not specifically mention those more general fundamentals here does not mean they are not relevant. Their significance is assumed. We wish only to focus the microscope on those things that will help us better teach and learn by the Spirit.

A Scriptural Comparison

From the very beginnings of my study on personal revelation and teaching by the Spirit, I knew that the question on the preceding page was a critical one that had to be addressed. As I began searching the scriptures for passages on personal revelation, including those on teaching, I began to notice something interesting. It was surprising to see how many references specifically taught:

- What things bring the Spirit into our lives, or
- What things grieve the Spirit and cause Him to withdraw.

I was so intrigued with that idea that I put these references into a DO and DON'T list to more clearly show how the Spirit works. I share it here with the recommendation that:

1. You read and study each reference for yourself rather than depend on the brief summaries given here.
2. Use this as a personal inventory checklist that you review regularly to remind you of what things will bring the Spirit more consistently into your life.
3. Try to think of (or remember) examples in your life, or maybe from the lives of others, that show real-life illustrations of each principle.

To Be in Closer Tune with the Spirit

- DO meditate on the word of God. (Joshua 1:8)
- DO NOT desire vain glory, provoke, or envy others. (Galatians 5:25–26)
- DO seek to bring forth Zion. (1 Nephi 13:37; see also 2 Nephi 26:29)
- DO NOT set yourself up as a light to the world. (2 Nephi 26:29)
- DO NOT set your heart upon gain or the praise of the world. (2 Nephi 26:29)
- DO NOT suppose that all you have to do is ask for an answer or solution. (D&C 9:7)

- DO study it out in your mind and make a decision, then ask if it is right. (D&C 9:8)
- DO desire to do much good, desiring in faith and with an honest heart. (D&C 11:8, 10, 17)
- DO seek to obtain the word before you teach. (D&C 11:21)
- DO NOT fear man; forget to rely on the Lord; focus too much on earthly things more than on God and your ministry; ignore the promptings of the Spirit or the counsel of your leaders; or be persuaded by those who are not doing God's will. (D&C 30:1–3)
- DO teach the doctrine, covenants, and church articles. (D&C 42:13)
- DO ask for the Spirit through the prayer of faith. (D&C 42:14)
- DO perform all that you do in the name of Christ. (D&C 46:31)
- DO give thanks for all your blessings. (D&C 46:32)
- DO practice virtue and holiness before God. (D&C 46:33)
- DO have a contrite spirit and speak with meekness so others are edified. (D&C 52:16)
- DO tremble (feel a sense of awe) under the power of God. (D&C 52:17)
- DO NOT seek to exalt yourself or refuse to be counseled. (D&C 63:55)
- DO speak with care of sacred things. (D&C 63:64)
- DO love God and purify yourself before Him. (D&C 76:116)
- DO treasure up the words of life continually. (D&C 84:85)
- DO seek God early. (D&C 88:83; see also D&C 54:10)
- DO declare His word with solemnity of heart in all meekness. (D&C 100:7–8)

- DO NOT seek to cover your sins, gratify your pride and vain ambitions, or exercise unrighteous dominion over others in any way. (D&C 121:37)
- DO seek to obtain the powers of heaven through persuasion, long-suffering, gentleness, love unfeigned, kindness, pure knowledge, eliminating hypocrisy, reproving when necessary but afterwards showing increased love, being full of charity, and letting virtue garnish your thoughts unceasingly. Doing these things brings the promise that the Holy Ghost shall be your constant companion. (D&C 121:41–46)

A careful study of this list, particularly if we use it as a way to evaluate our own spiritual standing, can be one of the most valuable things we can do to increase our sensitivity and ability to receive and recognize the Spirit as we teach.

CHAPTER 18

In Conclusion

Conversion

We have previously mentioned the new curriculum for the Aaronic Priesthood and Young Women programs, "Come Follow Me," that was recently initiated throughout the Church. The accompanying guide for teachers contains a letter of welcome from the First Presidency, addressed to "Beloved Parents, Teachers, Advisers, and Leaders of Youth." The opening line of that letter contains a charge to those listed in the greeting. It reads: "You are called by the Lord to *help youth become converted* to the gospel." In the next-to-last paragraph, they go on to say:

> Every worthy Latter-day Saint can teach the gospel in the Savior's way. As you follow His example, the Holy Ghost will help you know what to do. *Your own testimony will grow, your conversion will be deepened, and you will be strengthened to meet the challenges of life.*[1]

That is a wonderful promise, and it is reminiscent of one we have cited previously several times: "Wherefore, he that preacheth and he that receiveth, understand one another, and both are edified and rejoice together" (D&C 50:22).

That's how it works. When we preach and teach the gospel by the Spirit, as we are specifically commanded to do (see D&C 42:14), then edification results for both the teacher and the learner. Experiences that edify are more commonly called "spiritual experiences," and *spiritual experiences lead to true conversion.* Note what Elder M. Russell Ballard taught about the relationship between spiritual experiences and conversion.

> *It is not . . . enough for us to be convinced by the gospel; we must act and think so that we are converted by it. In contrast to the institutions of the world, which teach us to know something, the gospel of Jesus Christ challenges us to become something. . . . The gospel of Jesus Christ is a plan that shows us how to become what our Heavenly Father desires us to become.*
>
> DALLIN H. OAKS,
> *WITH FULL PURPOSE OF HEART*, 37–38

There is concern that some people in the Church have mental but not spiritual conversion. The gospel appeals to them, but real conversion is when they feel something in their hearts and not just in their minds. There is mental assent, but not spiritual conviction. *They must be touched by the power of the Holy Ghost, which creates a spiritual experience.* The power and deep conversion of the Spirit is needed by our members to get into their hearts to confirm what they agreed to in their minds. This will carry them through every storm of adversity. The great task, the great challenge of the First Presidency and the Twelve is *to get the spirit of the gospel from people's minds into their hearts, to where they have spiritual experiences, and those spiritual experiences are enough that they change feelings, they change our view of life.*[2]

How simple is our task, at least in concept. As we teach and minister by the Spirit, the Holy Ghost is invited to become part of the process. When the Holy Ghost is there and filling His functions, then spiritual experiences will naturally result. Such spiritual experiences increase testimony and strengthen faith, which leads to true conversion. When we are truly converted, then we can move forward on the path of life knowing that as long as we are faithful and endure to the end, we will return to the presence of God to live with Him and His Beloved Son for all eternity.

That is the importance of preaching and teaching by the Spirit. It is a crucial element in the entire process, and so are teachers of every kind and sort. The Lord has given the responsibility to save His children to teachers. The charge is clear. It is specific. It is inspiring. And, gratefully, the Lord blesses us greatly when we strive to carry out His will.

Let us now close this work with some final counsel from those we sustain as prophets, seers, and revelators.

Dallin H. Oaks. If we have the Spirit of the Lord to guide us, we can teach any person, no matter how well educated, any place in the world. The Lord knows more than any of us, and if we are his servants, acting under his Spirit, he can deliver his message of salvation to each and every soul.[3]

David A. Bednar. Parents and teachers need to do much more with the children and young people than say, essentially, "Sit down and pay attention while we tell you what you need to know." Parents and leaders should become guides who help young people learn how to find answers for themselves. Youth need to act as agents and properly exercise their agency in order to obtain and retain strong testimonies and to become converted—instead of primarily depending spiritually on someone else. We cannot borrow from another what is necessary "to stand as witnesses of God at all times and in all things, and in all places" (Mosiah 18:9). With multitudes of secular influences trying to counteract the truth about and from God, no one can thrive by attempting to borrow light from the spiritual lamps of others.[4]

Bruce R. McConkie. Now we want to carry this message to the world in the way that the Lord wants us to carry it. We want to preach the truth in purity and in perfection, and to do it in the way the Lord wants it done. The only single formula whereby we may do this is for us so to live . . . that we can be guided by the Holy Ghost. We must be guided by the Spirit. We have to have the Lord tell us how he wants us to teach the message of the restoration, and every doctrine of the gospel, and he will do this by revelation from the Holy Ghost if we are worthy to receive it. . . . We have no interest in teaching by the wisdom or learning or according to the precepts of men. We want to teach the gospel the way the Lord would have us teach it, and to do it under the power and influence of the Holy Ghost. If we will do that, we will teach sound doctrine. It will be the truth. It will build faith and increase righteousness in the hearts of men, and they will be led along that path which leads to the celestial world.[5]

Boyd K. Packer. I should like to close this book where we began—by acknowledging and paying homage to Him who is the Master Teacher. It is He who should be our ideal. No treatise on how to teach compares with a careful study of the four Gospels. Brief though they are, there is enough in these scriptures to open the doors to all the essential principles of teaching necessary to one who would succeed in teaching moral and spiritual values. The question might be asked, What manner of teacher ought we to be? Even as He is! In the course of my efforts to teach His gospel, I have come to know Him—Jesus Christ, the Son of God, the Only Begotten of the Father.[6]

With that counsel, let the final words on this subject be those of the Savior:

- Preach my gospel by the Spirit. (D&C 50:14)
- And the Spirit shall be given unto you by the prayer of faith; and if ye receive not the Spirit ye shall not teach. (D&C 42:14)
- I have prayed for thee, that thy faith fail not: and when thou art converted, strengthen thy brethren. (Luke 22:32)

Notes

Please note that in all scripture references throughout the book, the emphasis added is my own.

Chapter 1: "Go Ye Therefore, and Teach All Nations"

Chapter title: Matthew 28:19.

1. As cited by Dallin H. Oaks, "Gospel Teaching," 78.
2. Letter from the First Presidency, September 12, 2012.

Chapter 2: "If Ye Receive Not the Spirit Ye Shall Not Teach"

Chapter title: D&C 42:14.

1. Harold B. Lee, *Teachings,* 456.

Chapter 3: Preaching, Teaching, and Edifying

1. Taken from *Strong's Concordance* as given in the *LDS Reference Library 2005,* electronic version. For example, see Matthew 5:19.
2. *LDS Reference Library 2005,* electronic version. For example, see Matthew 4:17.
3. In Greek, a double *g* takes an "ng" sound, as in the word *angle.*

4. *LDS Reference Library 2005,* electronic version. For example, see Matthew 1:20.

5. *LDS Reference Library 2005,* electronic version. For example, see Acts 5:42.

6. MyEtymology.com, s.v. "edify."

7. Neal A. Maxwell, *Not My Will, but Thine,* 124.

CHAPTER 5: THE HOLY GHOST EDIFIES, STRENGTHENS, AND TESTIFIES

1. Spencer W. Kimball, *Faith Precedes the Miracle,* 85.

2. "Know This, That Every Soul Is Free," *Hymns,* no. 240.

CHAPTER 6: THE HOLY GHOST BESTOWS THE GIFTS OF THE SPIRIT, PART I

1. Bruce R. McConkie, *Mormon Doctrine,* 2nd ed., 314.

2. Stephen L Richards, *Where Is Wisdom?* 198–99.

3. Ardeth G. Kapp, "Taking upon Us His Name," 44.

CHAPTER 8: THE HOLY GHOST BESTOWS THE GIFTS OF THE SPIRIT, PART III

1. Joseph Smith, *Teachings,* 25.

2. Joseph Smith, *Teachings,* 162.

3. David O. McKay, in Clare Middlemiss, *Cherished Experiences,* 74.

CHAPTER 10: STRIVING AND ENLIGHTENMENT

1. Joseph Smith, *Teachings,* 328.

2. In my book *Hearing the Voice of the Lord,* 78–91, the topic of enlightenment is treated in greater detail, with additional examples of how the Spirit functions in giving us this enlightenment.

3. Dallin H. Oaks, *The Lord's Way,* 31–32.

CHAPTER 11: POWER AND AUTHORITY, REMEMBRANCE, AND KNOWING WHAT TO SAY IN THE VERY HOUR

1. Bible Dictionary, s.v. "Faith," 669.

2. Joseph Smith, *Teachings,* 148.

3. Joseph F. Smith, *Gospel Doctrine,* 13.

4. If taken literally, the command to "take no thought beforehand" seems like an odd thing for the Lord to say. This phrase, however, is also used in Matthew 6:25, 34. Footnote b to verse 25 says that the Greek word translated as *thought* means "anxious concern." So another way to say this might be, "Don't be overly concerned about what to say. Don't get all worried and stressed about it, for the Spirit is there to help you."

Chapter 12: An Increase in Skills and Abilities

1. The brother of Jared built eight separate barges that were tight "like unto a dish" (Ether 2:17), and Noah built a ship that was 300 cubits (450 feet) long, half again the length of an American football field (see Genesis 6:15).
2. Dallin H. Oaks, "Teaching and Learning by the Spirit," 7.

Chapter 13: Answering the Questions

1. See *Hearing the Voice of the Lord*, 235–60.
2. Boyd K. Packer, "Candle of the Lord," 55.

Chapter 14: Clarifying Misunderstandings

1. This is discussed at some length in *Hearing the Voice of the Lord*, 180–98.
2. Neal A. Maxwell, "Teaching by the Spirit," 2.
3. Dallin H. Oaks, "Teaching and Learning by the Spirit," 9.
4. Richard G. Scott, "Power of *Preach My Gospel*," 29–30.
5. Richard G. Scott, "Helping Others to Be Spiritually Led," 3.
6. "Use Effective Methods: Principles and Methods of Teaching," in "Leadership and Teaching" section at www.lds.org.

Chapter 15: Some Words of Caution

1. Jeffrey R. Holland, "We Are Teachers," 1.
2. The other one is D&C 33:4.
3. Holland, "We Are Teachers," 1.
4. But wait. What about seminary and institute teachers who are paid employees? What about speakers at Education Week or other

conferences, like Especially for Youth, who receive a stipend? Is this a form of priestcraft? No, because, as Elder Holland explained, they are not paid to preach, they are paid to educate. And what payment they do receive is modest in return for the investment they make in time and travel.

CHAPTER 16: "NOURISHED BY THE GOOD WORD OF GOD"

1. Gordon B. Hinckley, "Converts and Young Men," 47.
2. Dallin H. Oaks, "Gospel Teaching," 78.
3. *Teachings of Spencer W. Kimball,* 524.
4. See Bible Dictionary, s.v. "Faith," 669.
5. Richard G. Scott, "Helping Others to Be Spiritually Led," 3.
6. Boyd K. Packer, "Little Children," 17.

CHAPTER 18: IN CONCLUSION

1. *Teaching the Gospel in the Savior's Way,* 2.
2. Comments by Elder M. Russell Ballard at Martin's Cove, Wyoming, July 11, 2001. Used by permission of Elder Ballard.
3. Dallin H. Oaks, "Teaching and Learning by the Spirit," 7.
4. David A. Bednar, *Increase in Learning,* 70.
5. Bruce R. McConkie, in Conference Report, October 1949, 76.
6. Boyd K. Packer, *Teach Ye Diligently,* 359.

BIBLIOGRAPHY

Ballard, M. Russell. *Our Search for Happiness.* 1993.

Bednar, David A. *Increase in Learning.* 2011.

———. "Quick to Observe." *Ensign,* December 2006, 31–36.

———. "Seek Learning by Faith." Address to CES educators, February 3, 2006.

Benson, Ezra Taft. *The Teachings of Ezra Taft Benson.* 1988.

Christensen, Joe J. *One Step at a Time: Building a Better Marriage, Family, and You.* 1996.

Clark, J. Reuben, Jr. *The Charted Course of the Church in Education.* 1938.

Eyring, Henry B. *Because He First Loved Us.* 2002.

Faust, James E. *Finding Light in a Dark World.* 2004.

Hinckley, Gordon B. "Converts and Young Men." *Ensign,* May 1997, 47–50.

———. *Teachings of Gordon B. Hinckley.* 1997.

Holland, Jeffrey R. "We Are Teachers of the Gospel." Introduction to "An Evening with Elder Gordon B. Hinckley," September 1978. Manuscript in possession of author.

Hunter, Howard W. *The Teachings of Howard W. Hunter.* Edited by Clyde J. Williams. 1997.

Hymns of The Church of Jesus Christ of Latter-day Saints. 1985.

Kapp, Ardeth G. "Taking upon Us His Name," *New Era,* 1982, 38–46.

Kimball, Spencer W. *Faith Precedes the Miracle.* 1972.

———. *The Teachings of Spencer W. Kimball.* Edited by Edward L. Kimball. 1982.

Lee, Harold B. "Eternal Investments." Address to CES educators, February 10, 1989.

———. *The Teachings of Harold B. Lee.* Edited by Clyde J. Williams. 1996.

Lund, Gerald N. *Hearing the Voice of the Lord: Principles and Patterns of Personal Revelation.* 2007.

Maxwell, Neal A. *Deposition of a Disciple.* 1976.

———. *Not My Will, but Thine.* 1988.

———. "The Old Testament: Relevancy within Antiquity." Address to CES educators, 1979.

———. "Teaching by the Spirit—'The Language of Inspiration.'" CES Old Testament Symposium, 1991.

———. *Things as They Really Are.* 1978.

McConkie, Bruce R. *Doctrinal New Testament Commentary.* 3 vols. 1965–73.

———. "The Foolishness of Teaching." Address to CES educators, 1981.

———. *Mormon Doctrine.* 2nd ed. revised. 1966.

McKay, David O. *Stepping Stones to an Abundant Life.* 1971.

Middlemiss, Clare. *Cherished Experiences from the Life of President David O. McKay.* 1976.

Monson, Thomas S. *Live the Good Life.* 1988.

Oaks, Dallin H. "Gospel Teaching." *Ensign,* November 1999, 78–80.

———. *The Lord's Way.* 1991.

———. *Pure in Heart.* 1988.

———. "Teaching and Learning by the Spirit." *Ensign,* March 1997, 6–14.

———. *With Full Purpose of Heart.* 2002.

Packer, Boyd K. "The Candle of the Lord." *Ensign*, January 1983, 51–56.

———. "Little Children." *Ensign,* November 1986, 16–18.

———. *Teach Ye Diligently.* 2005.

Perry, L. Tom. "If Ye Receive Not the Spirit Ye Shall Not Teach." Address to CES educators, September 12, 1986.

Richards, Stephen L. *Where Is Wisdom?* 1955.

Scott, Richard G. "Helping Others to Be Spiritually Led." Address to CES educators, August 11, 1998.

———. "The Power of *Preach My Gospel.*" *Ensign*, May 2005, 29–31.

Smith, Joseph, Jr. *Teachings of the Prophet Joseph Smith.* Selected and arranged by Joseph Fielding Smith. 1976.

Smith, Joseph F. *Gospel Doctrine.* 1939.

Smith, Joseph Fielding. *Doctrines of Salvation.* 3 vols. Edited by Bruce R. McConkie. 1954–56.

Tanner, Susan W. "Did I Tell You . . . ?" *Ensign*, May 2003, 73–75.

Teaching the Gospel in the Savior's Way. 2012.

INDEX

———✦•✦———

Abilities: increased through Holy Ghost, 100–108; in teaching, 129–31

Abraham, 96–97, 113

Academic calendar, inspiration regarding, 87–88

Agency: in opening heart, 42–43, 118; and striving of Spirit, 78–79; in teaching, 118; of youths, 167

Aholiab, 102

Alma the Younger, 5–6

Apostles, and gift of tongues, 65–66

Application, teaching for, 147–48, 151

Arm wrestling, 81–82

Authority, through Holy Ghost, 89–92

Ballard, M. Russell: on Holy Ghost as testifier, 37; on spiritual experiences and conversion, 165–66

Bednar, David A.: on acceptance of gospel message, 43; on discernment, 51; on teaching children and youth, 166–67

Behavior, doctrine's effect on, 154

Belief, as spiritual gift, 54–57

Benson, Ezra Taft, 139

Bezaleel, 101–2

Bible, 119

Bishops, taught and magnified by Spirit, 101

Book of Mormon: examples of teaching in, 5–6; testimony of, 55–56; anti-Mormon rhetoric regarding, 116; priestcraft in, 135

Brigham Young University, inspiration regarding, 87–88

Broadcasting system, 7–8